Hamlyn
All Colour Book of
Main Dishes

Hamlyn
All Colour Book of

Main Dishes

Carol Bowen

HAMLYN

London · New York · Sydney · Toronto

Contents

For Peter

Photography by Paul Williams
Line illustrations by Marilyn Day

Published by
The Hamlyn Publishing Group Limited
London · New York · Sydney · Toronto
Astronaut House, Feltham, Middlesex, England

ISBN 0 600 32248 3

Phototypeset in Great Britain by Computer Photoset Limited.

Printed and bound in Spain
by Graficromo, S. A. – Córdoba

Useful facts and figures

Notes on metrication

In this book quantities are given in metric and Imperial measures. Exact conversion from Imperial to metric measures does not usually give very convenient working quantities and so the metric measures have been rounded off into units of 25 grams. The table below shows the recommended equivalents.

Ounces	Approx g to nearest whole figure	Recommended conversion to nearest unit of 25
1	28	25
2	57	50
3	85	75
4	113	100
5	142	150
6	170	175
7	198	200
8	227	225
9	255	250
10	283	275
11	312	300
12	340	350
13	368	375
14	396	400
15	425	425
16 (1 lb)	454	450
17	482	475
18	510	500
19	539	550
20 (1¼ lb)	567	575

Note When converting quantities over 20 oz first add the appropriate figures in the centre column, then adjust to the nearest unit of 25.

As a general guide, 1 kg (1000 g) equals 2.2 lb or about 2 lb 3 oz. This method of conversion gives good results in nearly all cases, although in certain pastry and cake recipes a more accurate conversion is necessary to produce a balanced recipe.

Liquid measures The millilitre has been used in this book and the following table gives a few examples.

Imperial	Approx ml to nearest whole figure	Recommended ml
¼ pint	142	150 ml
½ pint	283	300 ml
¾ pint	425	450 ml
1 pint	567	600 ml
1½ pints	851	900 ml
1¾ pints	992	1000 ml (1 litre)

Spoon measures All spoon measures given in this book are level unless otherwise stated.

Can sizes At present, cans are marked with the exact (usually to the nearest whole number) metric equivalent of the Imperial weight of the contents, so we have followed this practice when giving can sizes.

Flour Unless specified, either plain or self-raising flour can be used in the recipes. Seasoned flour is flour mixed with salt and freshly ground pepper.

10

Oven temperatures

The table below gives recommended equivalents.

	°C	°F	Gas Mark
Very cool	110	225	$\frac{1}{4}$
	120	250	$\frac{1}{2}$
Cool	140	275	1
	150	300	2
Moderate	160	325	3
	180	350	4
Moderately hot	190	375	5
	200	400	6
Hot	220	425	7
	230	450	8
Very hot	240	475	9

Notes for American and Australian users

In America the 8-oz measuring cup is used. In Australia metric measures are now used in conjunction with the standard 250-ml measuring cup. The Imperial pint, used in Britain and Australia, is 20 fl oz, while the American pint is 16 fl oz. It is important to remember that the Australian tablespoon differs from both the British and American tablespoons; the table below gives a comparison. The British standard tablespoon, which has been used throughout this book, holds 17.7 ml, the American 14.2 ml, and the Australian 20 ml. A teaspoon holds approximately 5 ml in all three countries.

British	American	Australian
1 teaspoon	1 teaspoon	1 teaspoon
1 tablespoon	1 tablespoon	1 tablespoon
2 tablespoons	3 tablespoons	2 tablespoons
$3\frac{1}{2}$ tablespoons	4 tablespoons	3 tablespoons
4 tablespoons	5 tablespoons	$3\frac{1}{2}$ tablespoons

An Imperial/American guide to solid and liquid measures

Solid measures

IMPERIAL	AMERICAN
1 lb butter or margarine	2 cups
1 lb flour	4 cups
8 oz rice	1 cup

Liquid measures

IMPERIAL	AMERICAN
$\frac{1}{4}$ pint liquid	$\frac{2}{3}$ cup liquid
$\frac{1}{2}$ pint	$1\frac{1}{4}$ cups
$\frac{3}{4}$ pint	2 cups
1 pint	$2\frac{1}{2}$ cups
$1\frac{1}{2}$ pints	$3\frac{3}{4}$ cups
2 pints	5 cups ($2\frac{1}{2}$ pints)

American terms

The list below gives some American equivalents or substitutes for terms and ingredients used in this book.

Equipment and terms
British/American
absorbent kitchen paper/paper towels
baking tray/baking sheet
cocktail stick/toothpick
deep cake tin/spring form pan
double saucepan/double boiler
dough or mixture/batter
flan tin/pie pan
frying pan/skillet
greaseproof paper/wax paper
grill/broil
loaf tin/loaf pan
minced/ground
patty or bun tins/muffin pans or cups
pudding basin/ovenproof bowl or pudding mold
roasting tin/roasting pan
stoned/pitted
whisk eggs/beat eggs

Ingredients
British/American
aubergine/eggplant
bacon rashers/bacon slices
beef fillet/ beef tenderloin
belly of pork/salt pork
black olives/ripe olives
black treacle/molasses
chicory/Belgian endive
chipolata sausages/link sausages
cooking apple/baking apple
cornflour/cornstarch
courgettes/zucchini
desiccated coconut/shredded coconut
double cream/heavy cream
gammon steaks/bacon steaks
gherkin/sweet dill pickle
hard-boiled egg/hard-cooked egg
haricot beans/navy beans
head of celery/bunch of celery
lard/shortening
minced beef/ground beef
natural yogurt/plain yogurt
ox tongue/beef tongue
pepper/sweet pepper
plain flour/all-purpose flour
self-raising flour/all-purpose flour sifted with baking powder
shortcrust pastry/basic pie dough
shredded beef suet/chopped beef suet
single cream/light cream
spring onions/scallions
stalks celery/sticks celery
sultanas/seedless white raisins
tomato purée/tomato paste
veal escalopes/veal scallops

NOTE: When making any of the recipes in this book, only follow one set of measures as they are not interchangeable.

Introduction

Ask any cook which is the most difficult course to plan and prepare and unreservedly it is most likely to be the main course! Juggling with varying and often opposing family tastes and preferences, conjuring with the seasonal availability of main meal ingredients and scheming to produce meals way ahead of dinner guests arriving can be quite a skilful art. It certainly isn't easy but it can be delicious with the ideas in this book.

There are main dish ideas to suit all occasions whether you want a simple but hearty family meal or superbly elegant dinner party dish. You could also try walking the culinary tightrope out of doors with enticing ideas for barbecues, picnics and patio meals. If you're a working wife or regularly entertain you'll also find the section on cook-ahead meals invaluable. Try cooking double the quantity and freeze one away for extra convenience and economy.

The ideal meal is a well-balanced meal, made up of the right dishes that can be produced without fluster. Often the easiest way to start is to choose the main course first, as it is usually the tricky one, then to add on a starter and a dessert. This book has been planned with this very much in mind so that you will have all the main dishes you're likely to need right at your fingertips.

All the recipes in this book are simple to prepare and have been double-tested by me, and by Bridget Jones, the Hamlyn home economist, who prepared all the dishes for the photographs. We both hope that you enjoy preparing and eating them and find them an inspiration for that most complicated course of all.

Carol Bowen

Quick Dishes

There are times when everyone needs a meal in a flash—a meal in the time it takes to spread a cloth on the lawn, set a tray, or draw the chairs up to the fire to watch television!

It won't be difficult to beat the clock with the recipes in this chapter. There are speedy ideas for every imaginable occasion from the quick midday working lunch to sumptuous formal dinner. The speedy solution may be in the form of a sauté dish like *Sizzling liver sauté* or *Cod and coriander sauté*. Sautéeing—to fry quickly until brown—has never been improved upon as a way of saving time, labour and fuel. It also captures the savoury juices of the meat or fish by 'surprising' the food with sudden heat and seals in the full flavour and colour of the ingredients used. Grills, like sautés, should also be considered—they both have that invaluable quality of adopting a variety of guises according to what food is in season, in the refrigerator, freezer or shop. Experiment with different herbs and spices, vegetables and meats for an expansible repertoire of quick dishes.

Take a tip too and wisely use those fast-working ingredients on the shelf of the store-cupboard—canned and dried foods as well as ready-prepared frozen foods. Pre-cooked and prepared they can save the day when time is at a premium.

Pan pizza and Apricot lamb butterflies (see overleaf)

Pan pizza

SERVES 3–4

DOUGH BASE
175 g/6 oz self-raising flour
pinch of salt
25 g/1 oz butter or margarine
75 ml/3 fl oz water
2 tablespoons oil

TOPPING
2 tablespoons tomato purée
1 (227-g/8-oz) can peeled tomatoes, drained
and roughly chopped
½ teaspoon dried oregano or marjoram
salt and freshly ground black pepper
75 g/3 oz Cheddar cheese, grated
1 (120-g/4¼-oz) can sardines in oil, drained
10 black olives

First make the dough base by sifting the flour with the salt. Rub in the fat until well incorporated then add the water to make a soft dough. Roll out on a lightly floured surface to a 25-cm/10-inch circle.

Heat the oil in a heavy-based 25-cm/10-inch frying pan. Add the pizza base and fry until golden on one side, about 5 minutes. (This can be cooked on an outdoor grill or barbecue or indoors on a conventional cooker). Turn the dough over and spread the tomato purée on the cooked side. Top with the tomatoes, herbs and seasoning. Sprinkle the cheese over and top with the sardines and olives, cook for about 7 minutes until the second side is golden brown. If liked, toast under a hot grill for 1–2 minutes. Serve hot in wedges from the pan.

Variation

Bacon and olive pan pizza
Prepare the pizza base as above. Spread 2 tablespoons tomato purée on the cooked side. Top with 1 (227-g/ 8-oz) can peeled tomatoes, drained and chopped; and ½ teaspoon dried mixed herbs. Cover with 225 g/8 oz crispy fried bacon rashers and 75 g/3 oz sliced Cheddar cheese. Garnish with 50 g/2 oz sliced stuffed olives. Cook as above.

Apricot and lamb butterflies

SERVES 4

4 lamb butterfly or Barnsley chops (saddle or
double loin chops)
1 (213-g/7½-oz) can apricot halves
1 teaspoon arrowroot powder
1 teaspoon Meaux mustard
1 tablespoon lemon juice
1 tablespoon clear honey
rosemary or parsley sprigs to garnish

Bake the chops in a roasting tin in a moderately hot oven (200°C, 400°F, Gas Mark 6) for 20–25 minutes or until cooked.

Meanwhile, drain the can of apricots but reserve the juice. Chop the apricots coarsely and place in a saucepan. Blend 200 ml/7 fl oz of the reserved apricot juice with the arrowroot powder and mustard. Pour over the apricots and stir well to mix. Add the lemon juice and honey. Cook over a gentle heat, stirring continuously until the sauce thickens and clears.

Serve the cooked chops coated with the apricot sauce and garnished with a few sprigs of parsley or rosemary.

Sizzling liver sauté

---------------- SERVES 4 ----------------

450 g/1 lb lamb's liver, thinly sliced
2 tablespoons Marsala or sweet sherry
salt and freshly ground black pepper
225 g/8 oz tomatoes, peeled and deseeded
2 tablespoons oil
2 small onions, thinly sliced
chopped parsley to garnish

Cut the liver into wafer-thin strips and place in a
shallow bowl with the Marsala or sherry. Add a liberal
quantity of black pepper and leave to marinate for 2–3
hours. Slice the tomatoes into thin strips and set aside.

Heat the oil in a frying pan. When hot, add the
strips of liver, a few at a time, and fry to cook quickly.
Remove from the pan and keep warm.

Add the onion to the pan juices and cook, covered, for
5 minutes. Stir in the marinade and seasoning to taste.
Replace the liver and add the tomato pieces. Bring to
the boil, check the seasoning and serve at once with
boiled rice. Garnish with chopped parsley.

Cod and coriander sauté

---------------- SERVES 4 ----------------

450 g/1 lb thick cut cod fillet
2 tablespoons flour
2 teaspoons ground coriander
salt and freshly ground white pepper
50 g/2 oz butter
1 tablespoon lemon juice
1 tablespoon capers
1 egg yolk
6 tablespoons single cream
lemon wedges to garnish

Skin the fish and divide into four pieces. Mix the
flour, coriander and a generous amount of seasoning
together. Coat the cod in this mixture.

Heat the butter in a medium-sized frying pan. When
hot and bubbling add the fish and fry gently until it is
golden on all sides, about 6–8 minutes. Add the lemon
juice and capers, cover and cook for 4–5 minutes, or
until the fish is tender. Transfer the fish to a warmed
serving dish.

Mix the egg yolk and cream together until well
blended. Stir into the pan juices and heat gently until
hot but not boiling. Adjust seasoning if necessary then
spoon over the fish and garnish with lemon wedges.

Chinese-style chicken

SERVES 4

4 tablespoons oil
100 g/4 oz cashew nuts
1 medium onion, chopped
350 g/12 oz raw chicken meat, cubed
50 g/2 oz mushrooms, chopped
1 green pepper, deseeded and chopped
1 carrot, thinly sliced
2 canned bamboo shoots, chopped
salt
2 teaspoons cornflour
2 teaspoons sugar
1 tablespoon soy sauce
2 teaspoons dry sherry
300 ml/$\frac{1}{2}$ pint chicken stock

Heat 1 tablespoon of the oil in a large frying pan and fry the cashews until golden brown. Remove from the pan. Add a further 2 tablespoons of the oil and fry the onion until crisp and transparent but not brown. Remove from the pan with a slotted spoon and reserve. Add the chicken and brown on all sides. Add the remaining oil, the vegetables and salt to taste. Cook, stirring occasionally, for 5–6 minutes.

Mix together the cornflour, a little salt, the sugar, soy sauce, sherry and stock in a small saucepan. Bring to the boil, stirring continuously, then pour over the chicken mixture. Add the nuts and onion and cook until very hot. Serve at once in warmed bowls with rice.

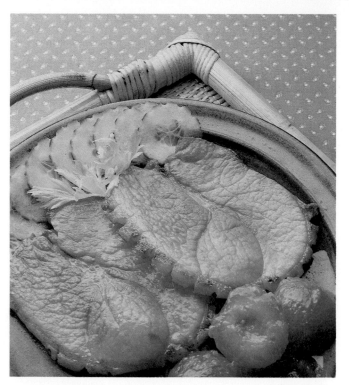

Gammon steaks with plum sauce

SERVES 4

4 gammon steaks
450 g/1 lb fresh plums, halved and stoned
300 ml/$\frac{1}{2}$ pint dry white wine or stock
25 g/1 oz cornflour
2 tablespoons clear honey
GARNISH
cucumber slices
celery leaves or parsley

Remove the rind from the gammon and snip at intervals down the edge of the fat. Cook under a preheated moderate grill until well cooked, about 8–12 minutes, turning frequently to ensure even cooking.

Meanwhile simmer the plums in the white wine for about 10 minutes until soft. Blend the cornflour with a little cold water, add to the plums and boil, stirring continuously until thickened. Stir in the honey and mix well.

Serve the sauce hot with the cooked gammon steaks and garnish with cucumber slices and celery leaves.

Variation

Gammon steaks with orange and redcurrant sauce
Blend 300 ml/$\frac{1}{2}$ pint orange juice with 4 tablespoons redcurrant jelly, 2 teaspoons cornflour and the grated rind of 1 orange. Bring to the boil, stirring, until slightly thickened. Simmer for 10 minutes before serving hot with the cooked gammon steaks.

Whiting pinwheels

SERVES 4

2 whiting, weighing about 350 g/12 oz each,
filleted
75 g/3 oz butter
2 tablespoons finely chopped fresh mixed herbs
(parsley, chives, balm or mint for example)
40 g/1½ oz fresh white breadcrumbs
grated rind and juice of 1 lemon
salt and freshly ground black pepper
GARNISH
lettuce leaves
twists of lemon
sprig of parsley

Grease a flameproof gratin dish. Skin the whiting fillets and cut each fillet in half lengthways to make a total of eight fish fillets.

Prepare the stuffing by beating the butter in a small bowl until soft and creamy. Add the herbs and breadcrumbs and stir in the lemon rind and enough lemon juice to make a spreading consistency. Season well and mix to blend. Divide the stuffing into eight portions and, using a round-bladed knife, spread each fillet lengthways with a portion of the stuffing. Roll up from the tail end and secure with a small skewer or wooden cocktail stick.

Place the prepared fish fillets in the gratin dish. Pour over any remaining lemon juice. Grill under a moderate heat for 5 minutes. Turn over, using a fish slice, and grill for a further 5–8 minutes. Serve at once on a bed of lettuce leaves and garnish with twists of lemon and a sprig of parsley.

Turkey breasts in cider cream sauce

SERVES 4

2 tablespoons oil
2 small onions, sliced
8 thin turkey fillets
2 tablespoons flour
400 ml/14 fl oz dry cider
salt and freshly ground black pepper
3 large red peppers, deseeded and sliced
150 ml/¼ pint double cream

Heat the oil in a frying pan. Add the onion and sauté until soft but not brown. Coat each turkey fillet in the flour. Add to the pan and cook on all sides until golden brown. Remove the turkey from the pan. Stir in any remaining flour and cook for 1 minute. Gradually add the cider, stirring continuously. Season to taste and bring to the boil.

Return the turkey to the pan with the red peppers. Reduce the heat and simmer for 15–20 minutes, or until the turkey is cooked. Remove from the heat and stir in the cream. Serve with buttered noodles and a green salad.

Sardine and tomato pizza

DOUGH BASE
100 g/4 oz self-raising flour
salt and freshly ground black pepper
25 g/1 oz butter or margarine
2 teaspoons dried mixed herbs
1 egg, beaten
milk to mix
TOPPING
25 g/1 oz butter
1 onion, sliced
2 tomatoes, peeled and sliced
1 (120-g/4¼-oz) can sardines in tomato sauce
75 g/3 oz Mozzarella cheese, sliced
GARNISH
1 black olive
1 tablespoon chopped parsley

Grease a baking tray. Prepare the pizza base by sifting the flour into a bowl with seasoning to taste. Rub in the butter or margarine until the mixture resembles fine breadcrumbs. Add the herbs, egg and sufficient milk to make a soft but workable dough. Shape into a 15-cm/6-inch round on the baking tray.

Melt the butter for the topping in a frying pan. Add the onion and cook until soft but not brown then spoon over the dough. Place the tomatoes on top and cover with the sardines and their sauce. Cover with the cheese and bake in a hot oven (230°C, 450°F, Gas Mark 8) for 15–20 minutes or until well risen and golden brown. Serve garnished with the olive and parsley.

Herby chicken goujons with cucumber sauce

4 (100-g/4-oz) chicken breasts, skinned and boned
seasoned flour to coat
1 egg, beaten
1 (85-g/3-oz) packet herb stuffing mix
3 tablespoons oil
25 g/1 oz butter
SAUCE
75 g/3 oz grated cucumber
150 ml/¼ pint mayonnaise
dash of Tabasco sauce
salt and freshly ground black pepper
1 teaspoon finely chopped parsley

Using a sharp knife, cut each chicken breast into six long strips. Coat in the seasoned flour and dip evenly in the beaten egg. Toss each chicken goujon in the dry herb stuffing mix.

Heat the oil and butter in a frying pan then, when hot, fry the goujons for 2–3 minutes on each side until cooked and golden brown. Drain on absorbent kitchen paper.

To make the sauce combine the cucumber, mayonnaise and Tabasco. Season to taste and transfer to a serving bowl. Sprinkle the top of the sauce with parsley and serve with the hot or cold goujons.

Variation

Herby chicken goujons with yogurt and onion sauce
Prepare the goujons as above. To make the sauce combine 75 g/3 oz finely-chopped onion with 150 ml/¼ pint natural yogurt and 1 crushed clove garlic. Season to taste and serve as above.

Veal vitello

SERVES 4–6

450 g/1 lb small thin slices of veal
seasoned flour to dust
100 g/4 oz prosciutto ham, thinly sliced
225 g/8 oz Mozzarella cheese, thinly sliced
few leaves of fresh sage or dried sage
salt and freshly ground black pepper
50 g/2 oz butter
50 g/2 oz Parmesan cheese, grated

Beat each slice of veal between two sheets of dampened greaseproof paper until wafer thin. Dust with the seasoned flour. Place a slice of prosciutto on each veal slice, top with several slices of Mozzarella, a little crushed fresh sage or dried sage and seasoning to taste. Roll up each veal slice and secure with a small skewer or wooden cocktail stick.

Melt the butter in a small flameproof gratin dish, add the rolled veal slices and sauté until brown on all sides, about 5–8 minutes. Sprinkle with the Parmesan and bake in a moderately hot oven (190°C, 375°F, Gas Mark 5) for 10 minutes. Serve at once with a crisp green salad.

Sausage and kidney ring

SERVES 4

50 g/2 oz butter
6 lamb's kidneys, cored and halved
1 large onion, chopped
100 g/4 oz streaky bacon, rind removed and chopped
100 g/4 oz mushrooms, sliced
15 g/½ oz seasoned flour
300 ml/½ pint brown ale
1 tablespoon tomato purée
salt and freshly ground black pepper
225 g/8 oz chipolata sausages
450 g/1 lb potatoes, boiled and mashed
2 (142-g/5-oz) cartons soured cream
chopped parsley to garnish

Melt half the butter in a frying pan. Add the kidneys and cook gently for about 5 minutes. Remove with a slotted spoon and keep warm. Add the remaining butter to the pan and melt. Add the onion, bacon and mushrooms and cook, over a low heat, for about 5 minutes. Stir in the flour, cook for 1 minute then gradually add the brown ale. Bring to the boil, stirring continuously. Add the tomato purée and season to taste. Simmer gently for about 5 minutes.

Meanwhile, grill the sausages until golden. Slice into thick pieces and add to the sauce with the cooked kidneys. Cook for a further 2 minutes.

Pipe or spoon the mashed potato around the edge of a flameproof serving dish or four individual dishes. Grill lightly to brown. Add the soured cream to the sausage mixture away from the heat and spoon into the potato 'nest'. Sprinkle with parsley and serve at once with seasonal vegetables.

Liver stroganoff

— SERVES 4 —

450 g/1 lb lamb's liver
40 g/1½ oz seasoned flour
75 g/3 oz butter
1 onion, finely chopped
2 rashers streaky bacon, rind removed and
chopped
100 g/4 oz mushrooms, finely sliced
150 ml/¼ pint stock
salt and freshly ground black pepper
1 (142-g/5-oz) carton soured cream
chopped chives to garnish

Cut the liver into 1-cm/½-inch strips and toss in the
seasoned flour. Heat half the butter in a frying pan
and sauté the liver until lightly browned, about 5
minutes. Remove with a slotted spoon and keep warm.
Add the remaining butter and heat to melt. Add the
onion, bacon and mushrooms. Cook until soft. Stir in
any remaining seasoned flour and cook for 1 minute.
Gradually pour in the stock and bring to the boil.
Season generously.

Return the liver to the pan and cook for a further 5
minutes. Remove from the heat and stir in the soured
cream. Garnish with chopped chives and serve with
boiled rice.

Speedy Spanish pork

— SERVES 4 —

450 g/1 lb pork fillet or pork tenderloin
1 tablespoon oil
25 g/1 oz butter
1 small onion, chopped
2 teaspoons flour
100 ml/4 fl oz red wine or stock
225 g/8 oz tomatoes, peeled, deseeded and
chopped
1 tablespoon tomato purée
1 clove garlic, crushed
salt and freshly ground black pepper
12 stuffed green olives, sliced

Cut the pork into eight thick pieces then beat out
thinly between sheets of dampened greaseproof paper to
make pork escalopes. Heat the oil and butter in a
large frying pan and brown the pork quickly on both
sides. Remove from the pan and keep warm.

Add the onion to the pan juices and brown lightly.
Stir in the flour and cook for 1 minute. Gradually add
the wine or stock and mix well to blend. Add the
tomatoes, tomato purée, garlic and seasoning to taste.
Bring to the boil, replace the pork escalopes and add
the olives. Cover and simmer for 10–15 minutes or
until the pork is tender.

Devilled kidneys

SERVES 4

1 tablespoon oil
15 g/½ oz butter
1 medium onion, finely chopped
100 g/4 oz streaky bacon, rind removed and
chopped
8 lamb's kidneys, cored and chopped
1 (227-g/8-oz) can peeled tomatoes
salt
1 teaspoon dried oregano
½ teaspoon cayenne pepper
1 tablespoon Worcestershire sauce
dash of Tabasco sauce
4 tablespoons medium sherry or stock
1 tablespoon chopped parsley to garnish

Heat the oil and butter together in a large frying pan.
Add the onion and bacon and sauté quickly until
golden. Add the kidneys and brown on all sides, about
5 minutes.

Stir in the tomatoes with their juice, salt to taste, the
oregano, cayenne, Worcestershire sauce, Tabasco and
sherry or stock. Bring to the boil, reduce the heat and
simmer for 10 minutes, stirring continuously. Check the
seasoning and serve with boiled rice or pasta, garnished
with the chopped parsley.

Chicken with curry mayonnaise

SERVES 4

575 g/1¼ lb cooked chicken meat
chopped parsley to garnish
CURRY MAYONNAISE
1 tablespoon oil
1 small onion, chopped
1 tablespoon curry powder
150 ml/¼ pint chicken stock
1 teaspoon tomato purée
juice of ½ lemon
2 tablespoons fruit chutney
300 ml/½ pint mayonnaise
3 tablespoons single cream

To make the mayonnaise, heat the oil in a small saucepan.
Add the onion and fry gently for 5 minutes. Stir in the
curry powder and cook for 2 minutes. Stir in the stock,
tomato purée, lemon juice and chutney. Bring to the
boil, reduce the heat and simmer for 5 minutes. Remove
from the heat and strain the sauce through a fine sieve
into a bowl. Allow to cool then stir in the mayonnaise
and single cream.

Remove any skin from the cooked chicken meat and
cut the meat into bite-sized pieces. Place in a serving dish
and coat with the curry mayonnaise. Sprinkle with
parsley and serve with a rice salad made up of cooked
rice, chopped green pepper, pineapple chunks, flaked
almonds and seedless raisins.

Pizza omelette

——— SERVES 2 ———

OMELETTE
4 eggs, beaten
salt and freshly ground black pepper
1 tablespoon cold water or milk
25 g/1 oz butter
TOPPING
25 g/1 oz butter
1 medium onion, chopped
2 teaspoons tomato purée
pinch of dried mixed herbs
4 rashers lean bacon, rind removed
75 g/3 oz Cheddar cheese, grated

Combine the eggs, seasoning to taste and water or milk and set aside.

Melt the butter for the topping in a saucepan. Add the onion and cook until soft, about 5 minutes. Add the tomato purée and herbs and cook for a further 2 minutes. Grill the bacon until crisp, crumble and set aside.

Melt the butter for the omelette in a 20-cm/8-inch heavy-based frying pan. Pour in the omelette mixture and cook, drawing the omelette mixture into the centre of the pan and allowing the uncooked mixture to flow to the outside of the pan. When set underneath, but still moist on top, remove the pan from the heat. Cover with the onion and tomato mixture, the bacon and finally the cheese.

Cook under a hot grill until the cheese melts and turns golden. Serve at once with a crisp salad.

Grilled steak with béarnaise sauce

——— SERVES 4 ———

4 fillet or rump steaks
50 g/2 oz butter
freshly ground black pepper
100 g/4 oz button mushrooms
3 tablespoons chopped parsley
BÉARNAISE SAUCE
1 teaspoon dried tarragon or 2 teaspoons chopped fresh tarragon
2 teaspoons chopped shallots or spring onions
salt and freshly ground black pepper
3 tablespoons wine vinegar
3 egg yolks
2 teaspoons water
100 g/4 oz butter

Place the steaks on a grill pan and dot with half the butter. Sprinkle with pepper to taste and grill under moderate heat for 6–10 minutes, turning halfway through, according to taste. Heat the remaining butter in a small saucepan and cook the mushrooms until tender, about 5 minutes. Add the parsley and keep warm.

Meanwhile prepare the sauce. Put the tarragon, chopped shallots or spring onions, seasoning and wine vinegar in a small saucepan. Boil over a moderate heat until reduced to 1 tablespoon. Transfer to a double boiler or to a bowl over a saucepan of simmering *not* boiling water. Stir in the egg yolks and water. Using a wire whisk, whisk in the butter, a few pieces at a time, until the sauce begins to thicken. Remove from the heat and serve with the cooked steaks and mushrooms.

Family Meals

Perhaps the most trying dish on a cook's calendar is the constantly repetitive family meal. Inspiration can run low even with meat, fish, poultry, cheese, pasta and eggs on the menu.

Gather cooking inspiration from the recipes to follow. The varied selection ranges from slow-cooking hearty casseroles, quick crumbles and risottos to traditional roasts and long-standing family favourites.

It is not surprising that a meal is often centred around the main course—nutritionally it needs to match up with the demands made for good health. It makes sound sense to plan a meal around the main course, choosing starter, dessert and vegetable or salad accompaniments to complement the main dish. But eating for good health needn't prove boring as the following recipes show. It will be easy to tickle the taste buds with *Honey-glazed chicken with banana*, *Steamed bacon pudding* or *Spaghetti with bacon sauce*.

A regular family meal also presents the cook with a splendid opportunity to introduce new flavours and foods to a willing audience. Even the most conservative of palates will be tempted to try *Tropical turkey paupiettes*, *Pork chops pizzaiola* and a touch of the Orient with *Sweet 'n' sour pork* or *Barbecued spareribs*. Mixed and matched with traditional English fare they make welcome alternatives and still use those readily available staples that don't cost the earth.

Brisket of beef with parsley dumplings;
Beef bake with herby choux topping
(see overleaf)

Brisket of beef with parsley dumplings

1 (1.4-kg/3-lb) salt beef brisket, soaked
overnight in cold water
225 g/8 oz carrots
2 medium onions
4 stalks celery
2 bay leaves
6 black peppercorns
300 ml/½ pint boiling water
PARSLEY DUMPLINGS
175 g/6 oz self-raising flour
1 teaspoon salt
2 teaspoons chopped parsley
75 g/3 oz shredded beef suet
cold water to mix

Line a roasting tin with greased aluminium cooking foil
and place the meat in the centre. Add the vegetables cut
into large chunks. Add the bay leaves, peppercorns and
water. Cover with a second piece of foil and secure
over the meat. Cook in a moderately hot oven (200°C,
400°F, Gas Mark 6) for 1 hour 50 minutes.

Meanwhile prepare the dumplings. Sift the flour and
salt into a bowl. Stir in the parsley and suet and mix to a
soft but workable dough with cold water. Divide the
mixture into eight portions and form into small dumplings.

Remove the foil from the meat, place the dumplings on
top of the vegetables, cover again with the foil and
continue cooking for 40 minutes until the dumplings
are well risen and cooked.

To serve, arrange the beef on a warmed serving dish.
Surround with the vegetables and dumplings. Slice the
meat thickly to serve.

Variations

Brisket of beef can be served with a variety of different
flavoured dumplings:
Bacon dumplings: Add 50 g/2 oz crispy fried bacon to the
above dumpling recipe.
Mustard dumplings: Add 2 teaspoons dry mustard
powder to the above recipe.
Herby dumplings: Add 1 teaspoon dried mixed herbs to
the above dumpling recipe.

Beef bake with herby choux topping

50 g/2 oz butter
1 large onion, sliced
450 g/1 lb braising steak, cubed
150 ml/¼ pint beef stock
450 g/1 lb tomatoes, peeled and deseeded
2 tablespoons tomato purée
300 ml/½ pint brown ale
salt and freshly ground black pepper
8 rashers back bacon, rind removed
HERBY CHOUX TOPPING
150 ml/¼ pint water
50 g/2 oz butter
75 g/3 oz plain flour
pinch of salt
2 eggs, beaten
25 g/1 oz mature Cheddar cheese, grated
½ teaspoon dried mixed herbs

Melt the butter in a frying pan. Add the onion and cook
for about 5 minutes until soft. Add the beef and cook
until browned on all sides. Transfer to a 1.75-litre/3-pint
casserole dish. Add the stock to the pan juices with the
tomatoes, tomato purée and brown ale. Season to taste
and mix well.

Cut the bacon rashers in half and roll up. Secure with
wooden cocktail sticks and grill, under a high heat, for
3–4 minutes until crisp. Remove the cocktail sticks and
place the bacon rolls in the casserole. Cover and cook in a
moderate oven (160°C, 325°F, Gas Mark 3) for 1¾ hours.

Meanwhile prepare the topping. Place the water in a
saucepan with the butter and heat gently until the
butter melts. Bring to the boil. Sift the flour with the
salt and add, all at once, to the water mixture. Beat
quickly to form a smooth choux paste. Cool until warm.
Gradually add the eggs, beating well to incorporate.
Add the cheese and herbs and seasoning to taste. Place
the mixture in a piping bag fitted with a large plain
nozzle and pipe choux buns around the edge of the
casserole.

Raise the oven temperature to hot (220°C, 425°F,
Gas Mark 7) and bake, uncovered, for 20 minutes.
Reduce the oven temperature to moderate (180°C,
350°F, Gas Mark 4) and cook for a further 20 minutes.

Variation

Beef bake with cheesy choux topping
Omit the herbs from the above herby choux topping
recipe. Prepare as above and pipe choux buns around
the edge of the casserole. Sprinkle the tops of the buns
with an extra 25 g/1 oz grated Cheddar cheese. Cook as
above.

Stuffed cod cutlets

———— SERVES 4 ————

4 cod cutlets, central bones removed
25 g/1 oz butter
1 small onion, chopped
4 rashers streaky bacon, rind removed and
chopped
2 tomatoes, peeled and chopped
25 g/1 oz fresh white breadcrumbs
4 tablespoons milk
salt and freshly ground black pepper

Place the cod cutlets on four pieces of greased aluminium cooking foil. Melt the butter in a small saucepan. Add the onion and bacon and fry until golden, about 8 minutes. Add the tomato and breadcrumbs and mix well to blend. Fill the centre of each cod cutlet with this mixture. Top each with a tablespoon of milk and season to taste. Fold over the foil to enclose completely.

Bake in a moderate oven (180°C, 350°F, Gas Mark 4) for about 20–25 minutes until cooked. Remove from the foil and serve.

Piquant stuffed trout

———— SERVES 2 ————

2 medium trout, gutted and cleaned
15 g/$\frac{1}{2}$ oz almonds, coarsely chopped
50 g/2 oz fresh white breadcrumbs
1 tablespoon chopped parsley
grated rind and juice of $\frac{1}{2}$ small lemon
1 egg, beaten
salt and freshly ground black pepper
150 ml/$\frac{1}{4}$ pint white wine
$\frac{1}{2}$ teaspoon dried tarragon
25 g/1 oz flaked almonds
15 g/$\frac{1}{2}$ oz butter

Place the trout in a shallow ovenproof dish. Mix the chopped almonds in a bowl with the breadcrumbs, parsley, lemon rind and juice. Bind together with the egg. Season to taste and use to stuff the cavities of the trout.

Mix the white wine and dried tarragon together and pour over the trout. Fry the flaked almonds in a small pan in the melted butter and sprinkle over the trout. Cover with greased aluminium cooking foil and bake in a moderate oven (180°C, 350°F, Gas Mark 4) for 20 minutes. Remove the foil and cook for a further 10 minutes.

Lamb bourguignonne

— SERVES 6 —

1.25 kg/2½ lb boned lean leg of lamb (boned
weight)
350 g/12 oz button onions
3 tablespoons oil
50 g/2 oz butter or margarine
225 g/8 oz button mushrooms
250 ml/8 fl oz dry red wine
300 ml/½ pint brown stock
½ teaspoon salt
freshly ground black pepper
1 tablespoon arrowroot powder
1 tablespoon water
GARNISH
chopped parsley
fried bread croûtons

Cut the meat into bite-sized pieces. Blanch the peeled
onions in boiling water for 2 minutes then drain.

Heat the oil in a large deep frying pan. Add the butter
or margarine and, when foaming, add the meat and
brown quickly on all sides. Remove with a slotted spoon
and reserve. Add the onions to the pan and brown
evenly. Remove with a slotted spoon and reserve.
Finally fry the mushrooms in the pan juices. Return the
lamb and onions to the pan. Stir in the wine, stock and
seasoning. Bring to the boil then transfer to a flameproof
casserole. Cover and cook in a moderate oven (160°C,
325°F, Gas Mark 3) for about 1½ hours or until the meat is
cooked. Remove the casserole from the oven.

Dissolve the arrowroot in the water, add slowly to the
casserole and cook for a further 5 minutes over a gentle
heat until the stock is clear and thickened. Adjust the
seasoning and serve garnished with chopped parsley
and fried bread croûtons.

Tropical turkey paupiettes

— SERVES 4 —

4 thin turkey escalopes
salt and freshly ground black pepper
225 g/8 oz pork sausagemeat
2 tablespoons mango chutney
25 g/1 oz salted peanuts, chopped
1 tablespoon oil
25 g/1 oz butter
225 g/8 oz parsnips, sliced
2 medium onions, sliced
2 teaspoons ground cumin
1 teaspoon dried rosemary
5 teaspoons flour
5 teaspoons desiccated coconut
250 ml/8 fl oz chicken stock
1 tablespoon chopped parsley

Beat out the escalopes between sheets of dampened
greaseproof paper until very thin. Season generously.

Mix the sausagemeat with 1 tablespoon of the chutney,
the nuts and seasoning to taste. Divide into four portions
and spread over the turkey escalopes. Roll up like a
Swiss roll and secure with wooden cocktail sticks.

Heat the oil and butter in a shallow flameproof
casserole. Brown the turkey paupiettes on all sides.
Remove from the casserole with a slotted spoon and
reserve. Add the parsnips, onion, cumin, rosemary,
flour and coconut to the pan juices and fry for 2–3
minutes. Gradually stir in the stock to make a thickened
sauce. Add the remaining chutney, the parsley and
seasoning to taste. Bring to the boil, replace the paupiettes in a single layer. Cover and cook in a cool oven
(150°C, 300°F, Gas Mark 2) for 1½ hours. Remove the
cocktail sticks and skim before serving with rice.

Apricot-stuffed lamb

SERVES 6

1 (1.8-kg/4-lb) shoulder of lamb, boned
salt and freshly ground black pepper
25 g/1 oz dripping or lard
1 onion, sliced
1 carrot, sliced
1 bay leaf
300 ml/½ pint stock
STUFFING
50 g/2 oz fresh white breadcrumbs
pinch of dried thyme
25 g/1 oz walnuts, chopped
1 small onion, chopped
1 tablespoon oil
1 (213-g/7½-oz) can apricots
1 egg, beaten

Season the lamb generously with salt and pepper and set aside whilst preparing the stuffing. Place the breadcrumbs, thyme and walnuts in a bowl. Fry the onion in the oil in a small saucepan until soft but not brown, about 5 minutes, and then add to the breadcrumb mixture. Drain and coarsely chop the apricots and stir into the stuffing mixture. Season to taste and bind with sufficient beaten egg to make a moist stuffing. Spoon the stuffing along the shoulder joint and tie with string into a long neat shape.

Heat the dripping or lard in a flameproof casserole and brown the meat on all sides. Add the sliced onion, carrot and bay leaf. Pour over the stock and bring to the boil. Cover and cook in a moderate oven (180°C, 350°F, Gas Mark 4) for 1½ hours, or until cooked.

To serve, remove the string from the lamb and place on a serving dish. Sieve the stock juices and pour over the lamb. Carve into thick slices and serve.

Crispy chicken with celery sauce

SERVES 4

4 chicken quarters, skinned
1 egg, beaten
salt and freshly ground black pepper
100 g/4 oz fine dry breadcrumbs
oil for deep frying
watercress sprigs to garnish
SAUCE
1 head of celery, weighing about 275 g/10 oz,
coarsely chopped
300 ml/½ pint milk
25 g/1 oz butter
15 g/½ oz flour
1 bunch watercress, trimmed and chopped
2 tablespoons single cream (optional)

Coat the chicken in beaten egg and then in the well-seasoned breadcrumbs. Set aside whilst preparing the sauce.

Place the celery in a medium-sized saucepan with the milk, season generously, cover and cook until tender, about 12–15 minutes. Pass through a sieve or blend in a liquidiser and then sieve to give a smooth celery purée.

Melt the butter in a clean saucepan. Add the flour and cook for 1 minute. Gradually stir in the celery purée to make a smooth sauce. Stir in the watercress and the cream if used. Check the seasoning and keep warm.

Deep fry the chicken pieces in hot oil until cooked, about 12–15 minutes. Drain on absorbent kitchen paper then garnish with watercress and serve at once with the celery sauce.

St Clement's mackerel

2 oranges, peeled and coarsely chopped
½ onion, chopped
50 g/2 oz fresh white breadcrumbs
1 tablespoon chopped parsley
finely grated rind of 1 lemon
2 tablespoons lemon juice
salt and freshly ground black pepper
4 medium mackerel, gutted and cleaned
GARNISH
1 orange, sliced
sprigs of parsley

Mix the orange, onion, breadcrumbs, parsley, lemon rind and juice together in a small bowl. Season to taste. Fill the cavities of the fish with the stuffing. Line a shallow ovenproof dish with greased aluminium cooking foil. Place the fish on the foil. Wrap the foil loosely around the fish and bake in a moderate oven (160°C, 325°F, Gas Mark 3) for 35 minutes. Serve at once, garnished with halved orange slices and sprigs of parsley.

Variation

Fruit 'n' nut mackerel
Mackerel is just as delicious stuffed with a piquant mixture of hazelnuts and grapefruit. Mix the coarsely-chopped flesh of 1 grapefruit with 50 g/2 oz fresh breadcrumbs, 1 tablespoon chopped parsley, the finely-grated rind of 1 lemon, 2 tablespoons lemon juice, 75 g/3 oz chopped, toasted hazelnuts and seasoning to taste. Fill the cavities of the fish with the stuffing and cook as above.

Norfolk fish pie

675 g/1½ lb cod or haddock fillet
600 ml/1 pint milk
150 ml/¼ pint water
225 g/8 oz carrots, thinly sliced
2 leeks, thinly sliced
50 g/2 oz butter
50 g/2 oz flour
2 teaspoons dry mustard powder
2 tablespoons chopped parsley
salt and freshly ground black pepper
450 g/1 lb tomatoes, peeled and thinly sliced
450 g/1 lb potatoes, boiled and mashed

Place the fish in a saucepan with 150 ml/¼ pint of the milk and the water. Bring to the boil and simmer for 10 minutes. Remove the fish from its cooking liquid, discard any bones and flake into large chunks. Reserve the cooking liquid.
Cook the carrot and leek in boiling, salted water for 10 minutes until tender. Drain and add to the fish.
Melt the butter in a saucepan. Add the flour and cook for 1 minute. Gradually add the remaining milk and reserved cooking liquid to make a smooth sauce. Add the mustard, parsley and seasoning to taste. Fold the fish and vegetables into the sauce then turn into a 1.25-litre/2-pint ovenproof dish. Top with a layer of sliced tomatoes.
Place the mashed potato in a piping bag fitted with a large star vegetable nozzle. Pipe swirls of potato on top of the fish mixture. Bake in a moderately hot oven (200°C, 400°F, Gas Mark 6) for 15–20 minutes or until golden.

Variation

Norfolk smoked fish pie
Substitute the cod or haddock fillet in the above recipe for 675 g/1½ lb smoked haddock, smoked cod or smoked trout for a delicious alternative dish.

Aubergine and bean casserole

— SERVES 4 —

3 tablespoons oil
2 onions, sliced
4 carrots, sliced
2 stalks celery, chopped
900 g/2 lb middle neck of lamb, cubed
seasoned flour to coat
1 large aubergine, weighing about 225 g/8 oz,
sliced
450 ml/¾ pint stock
100 g/4 oz dried haricot beans, soaked overnight
in cold water
1 tablespoon tomato purée
salt and freshly ground black pepper
chopped parsley to garnish

Heat the oil in a large flameproof casserole and sauté the onion, carrot and celery for about 5 minutes. Remove from the pan with a slotted spoon and set aside.

Coat the lamb in seasoned flour and add to the pan juices. Quickly fry until well browned. Return the vegetables to the casserole. Add the aubergine, pour over the stock and mix in the drained beans. Stir in the tomato purée and season to taste.

Bring to the boil, cover and simmer for 2½ hours until the meat and beans are tender. Allow to cool, skim away any surface fat then reheat for 15–20 minutes. Serve garnished with chopped parsley and accompany with a crisp salad and jacket potatoes.

Chicken pilaf

— SERVES 6 —

50 g/2 oz butter
25 g/1 oz flour
1 (426-ml/15-fl oz) can evaporated milk or
400 ml/14 fl oz milk
300 ml/½ pint stock
salt and freshly ground black pepper
450 g/1 lb cooked chicken meat, cut into bite-
sized pieces
450 g/1 lb cooked long-grain rice (about
225 g/8 oz uncooked weight)
100 g/4 oz button mushrooms, sliced
1 green pepper, deseeded and chopped
1 red pepper, deseeded and chopped
1 tablespoon chopped parsley

Melt the butter in a medium-sized saucepan. Add the flour and cook for 1 minute. Gradually stir in the evaporated milk or ordinary milk and the stock to make a smooth sauce. Bring to the boil and simmer for 2 minutes. Season to taste.

Fold in the chicken, rice, mushrooms, peppers and parsley. Turn into a 1.75-litre/3-pint casserole dish. Cover and cook in a moderate oven (180°C, 350°F, Gas Mark 4) for 45 minutes. Adjust the seasoning if necessary and serve.

Shepherd's pie with cheesy potato topping

SERVES 4–6

15 g/½ oz butter
2 tablespoons oil
1 medium onion, finely chopped
450 g/1 lb cooked roast beef, minced
150 ml/¼ pint rich beef gravy
2 teaspoons Worcestershire sauce
1 tablespoon chopped parsley
¼ teaspoon dried mixed herbs
salt and freshly ground black pepper
TOPPING
6 tablespoons double cream
40 g/1½ oz butter, melted
2 eggs, lightly beaten
900 g/2 lb potatoes, boiled and mashed
75 g/3 oz Cheddar cheese, grated

Grease a deep 1.75-litre/3-pint ovenproof dish with the butter. Heat the oil in a saucepan. Add the onion and sauté for 5 minutes. Stir in the beef, gravy, Worcestershire sauce, parsley, herbs and seasoning to taste. Place in the dish.

Beat the cream, 25 g/1 oz of the butter and the eggs into the hot mashed potato. Add the cheese, mix to blend and season to taste. Pipe or spoon the mashed potato on top of the meat mixture and brush with the remaining melted butter.

Bake in a moderately hot oven (200°C, 400°F, Gas Mark 6) for 20–25 minutes until puffed and golden brown.

Courgette baked chicken

SERVES 4

4 chicken portions or drumsticks
salt and freshly ground black pepper
50–75 g/2–3 oz butter
1 tablespoon finely chopped parsley
juice of ½ lemon
450 g/1 lb courgettes, thickly sliced
chopped parsley to garnish

Grease a shallow roasting tin. Season the chicken generously. Cream the butter until soft, then beat in the chopped parsley and lemon juice. Spread thickly over the chicken portions and bake in a moderate oven (180°C, 350°F, Gas Mark 4) for 1 hour.

Meanwhile, pare the courgettes and blanch in boiling salted water for 15 minutes. Add to the chicken 15 minutes before the end of the cooking time. Turn and baste the courgettes in the melted parsley butter.

Serve the chicken surrounded with the courgettes and with the pan juices poured over. Garnish with the parsley.

Pork chops pizzaiola

SERVES 6

1 teaspoon salt
1 teaspoon freshly ground black pepper
6 pork loin chops, cut 2 cm/¾ inch thick
3 tablespoons oil
2 cloves garlic, crushed
1 teaspoon dried basil
1 teaspoon dried thyme
1 bay leaf
75 ml/3 fl oz dry red wine or dark stock
1 (425-g/15-oz) can peeled tomatoes, drained
and finely chopped
2 tablespoons tomato purée
40 g/1½ oz butter
3 medium green peppers, deseeded and finely
chopped
1 medium onion, sliced in rings
225 g/8 oz button mushrooms (optional)
1½ tablespoons cornflour

Rub the salt and pepper into both sides of the pork chops. Set aside.

In a large frying pan, heat the oil until hot, add the chops and brown for 3 minutes on each side. Remove with a slotted spoon and set aside.

Add the garlic, basil, thyme and bay leaf to the pan. Pour in the wine or stock and bring to the boil. Add the tomatoes and tomato purée. Return the pork chops to the pan and baste thoroughly with the sauce. Cover and simmer for 40 minutes, basting from time to time.

Meanwhile melt the butter in a medium-sized frying pan. Add the peppers and onion. Cook, stirring occasionally, for 5–10 minutes. Add the mushrooms, if used, and cook for a further 2–3 minutes.

Add these vegetables to the pork chop mixture and continue to cook, uncovered, for a further 15 minutes.

To serve, remove the pork chops from the pan and place in a warmed serving dish. Thicken the sauce with the cornflour, dissolved in a little water, and pour over the pork chops. Serve with boiled noodles.

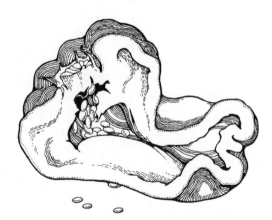

Roast pork with apple and nut stuffing

SERVES 6

25 g/1 oz butter
1 small onion, chopped
50 g/2 oz cashew nuts, coarsely chopped
50 g/2 oz crustless white bread, diced
1 cooking apple, peeled, cored and diced
1 stalk celery, chopped
2 teaspoons chopped parsley
salt and freshly ground black pepper
2 teaspoons lemon juice
1 (1.5-kg/3½-lb) blade or loin of pork, boned
2–3 tablespoons oil
150 ml/¼ pint dry cider

Melt the butter in a small pan and fry the onion and nuts until they both just turn colour, about 5 minutes. Add the bread, apple, celery and parsley. Continue to cook for about 5 minutes or until the apple softens. Season to taste and add the lemon juice.

Deeply score the rind of the pork evenly. Open up the pocket in the blade joint and spread evenly with the stuffing. Alternatively place the stuffing in the loin. Roll up and secure with string. Place in a greased roasting tin. Brush with the oil and sprinkle generously with salt. Roast in a moderately hot oven (200°C, 400°F, Gas Mark 6) for 20–30 minutes, until the crackling is crisp and golden. Reduce the oven temperature to moderate (180°C, 350°F, Gas Mark 4) and cook for a further 1½ hours.

Place the pork on a warmed serving dish and keep warm. Skim away any fat from the meat juices in the roasting tin. Add the cider, bring to the boil and simmer for 5 minutes, stirring well to incorporate any meat residue. Season to taste and serve with the pork.

Cook's Tip

One of the delicious delights of roast pork is the crisp golden crackling that is produced when the rind is left in place. To ensure a crunchy golden crust but succulent interior, score the rind with a sharp knife at regular intervals taking care not to penetrate the flesh. Place in a roasting pan and smear with oil. Sprinkle with salt and rub into the incisions. Cook initially in a moderately hot oven (200°C, 400°F, Gas Mark 6) for 30 minutes to crisp the skin then reduce the temperature to moderate (180°C, 350°F, Gas Mark 4) and cook for the remainder of the cooking time (allow 25 minutes per 450 g/1 lb).

Honey-glazed chicken with banana

1 (1.4-kg/3-lb) oven-ready chicken
1 tablespoon oil
4 tablespoons clear honey
$\frac{1}{2}$ teaspoon prepared mustard
1 tablespoon Worcestershire sauce
freshly ground black pepper
2 firm bananas, sliced
watercress sprigs to garnish

Cut the chicken in half through the breast bone. Lightly oil a roasting tin. Combine the honey, mustard, Worcestershire sauce and pepper to taste in a small bowl. Place the chicken halves, skin side up, in the tin. Brush with the honey marinade and cook in a moderately hot oven (200°C, 400°F, Gas Mark 6) for 40 minutes, or until cooked. Brush with the marinade frequently.

When cooked, pour any pan juices from the chicken, free of excess fat, into a small saucepan. Add the bananas and heat through just enough to warm the bananas. Spoon over the chicken and serve garnished with watercress.

Variation

Caribbean glazed chicken with banana
Prepare the chicken as above but marinate for 30 minutes in a combined mixture of 4 tablespoons dark rum, 4 tablespoons soy sauce, 4 tablespoons lime juice and seasoning to taste. Cook as above brushing the chicken with the marinade.

Chicken tetrazzini

175 g/6 oz spaghetti
175 g/6 oz collar bacon, rind removed and cut into 1-cm/$\frac{1}{2}$-inch pieces
225 g/8 oz cooked chicken meat, cut into bite-sized pieces
1 (198-g/7-oz) can sweet red peppers, sliced
40 g/1$\frac{1}{2}$ oz butter
40 g/1$\frac{1}{2}$ oz flour
150 ml/$\frac{1}{4}$ pint milk
450 ml/$\frac{3}{4}$ pint chicken stock
75 g/3 oz Cheddar cheese, grated
salt and freshly ground black pepper
$\frac{1}{4}$ teaspoon ground nutmeg
2 tablespoons sherry
1 egg yolk, beaten
25 g/1 oz flaked almonds

Cook the spaghetti in a large pan of boiling salted water until cooked – about 10–12 minutes.

Fry the bacon gently in a large pan until crisp but not brown. Add the chicken and peppers and cook for a further 5 minutes. Stir in the cooked drained spaghetti and remove from the heat.

Melt the butter in a medium-sized saucepan, add the flour and cook for 1 minute. Gradually stir in the milk and stock to make a smooth sauce. Bring to the boil, stirring continuously, and allow the sauce to thicken. Add the cheese, seasoning to taste, nutmeg and sherry. Remove from the heat and stir in the egg yolk.

Place the chicken and pasta mixture in an ovenproof dish and coat with the sauce. Sprinkle with the flaked almonds and heat through in a moderately hot oven (190°C, 375°F, Gas Mark 5) for about 25 minutes until lightly browned.

Cook's Tip

Pasta will not stick together during cooking or before serving if you add 1 teaspoon oil to the cooking water. After cooking rinse in the normal way.

Gingered lemon chops

SERVES 4

150 ml/¼ pint olive oil
grated rind of 2 lemons
4 tablespoons lemon juice
2 tablespoons soft brown sugar
1 teaspoon ground ginger
1 teaspoon grated fresh root ginger
2 teaspoons ginger wine
salt and freshly ground black pepper
4 large lamb loin or chump chops
GARNISH
watercress sprigs
lemon wedges

Mix the oil, lemon rind, lemon juice, sugar, ground ginger, root ginger, ginger wine and seasoning to taste in a small bowl. Place the lamb chops in a shallow dish. Pour over the marinade and leave for 2–3 hours, turning the chops frequently in the marinade mixture.

Place on a grill pan and cook under a moderate grill for 15 minutes, turning halfway through the cooking time and basting regularly with the marinade. Garnish with watercress and lemon wedges.

Steamed bacon pudding

SERVES 4–6

450 g/1 lb streaky bacon, rind removed
350 g/12 oz self-raising flour
salt and freshly ground black pepper
100 g/4 oz butter or margarine
100 g/4 oz onion, grated
1 teaspoon dried mixed herbs
1 tablespoon finely chopped parsley
2 large eggs, beaten
175 ml/6 fl oz cold milk

Stretch 8–10 of the bacon rashers with the back of a knife and use to line a lightly greased 1.25-litre/2-pint pudding basin. Chop the rest of the bacon finely.

Sift the flour and a little seasoning into a bowl. Rub the butter or margarine in finely, add the chopped bacon, onion, herbs and parsley. Gradually add the eggs and the milk to make a stiff batter. Turn into the prepared basin and cover securely with a sheet of buttered and pleated greaseproof paper and aluminium cooking foil. Steam for 2 hours over simmering water.

To serve, turn out onto a warmed serving dish and accompany with onion gravy and apple sauce.

Pork and cider casserole

SERVES 4

4 pork chops
1 medium onion, sliced
15 g/½ oz seasoned flour
1 teaspoon chopped fresh sage
or ½ teaspoon dried sage
salt and freshly ground black pepper
150 ml/¼ pint stock
150 ml/¼ pint dry cider
1 cooking apple, cored
2 tomatoes, peeled and sliced

Place the chops in a heavy-based pan and set over a low heat until the fat runs. Increase the heat and cook until the chops are lightly browned on both sides, about 10 minutes. Add the onion and cook for 5 minutes. Drain off any surplus fat. Shower in the flour and cook for 1 minute. Add the sage and seasoning then gradually stir in the stock and cider. Bring to the boil, then cover and cook in a moderate oven (160°C, 325°F, Gas Mark 3) for 1 hour.

Cut the apple into thick rings and arrange over the chops. Place the tomatoes on top of the apple and continue to cook for a further 10 minutes so that the top becomes soft.

Seafood paella

SERVES 4–6

2 chicken portions, skinned
3 tablespoons oil
225 g/8 oz lean pork, cubed
1 (225-g/8-oz) piece garlic sausage, cubed
1 medium onion, chopped
3 tomatoes, peeled and chopped
450 g/1 lb long-grain rice
225 g/8 oz shelled peas
1 red pepper, deseeded and chopped
salt and freshly ground black pepper
pinch of powdered saffron or turmeric
900 ml/1½ pints stock
2 tablespoons chopped parsley
225 g/8 oz peeled prawns
12–15 cooked mussels or canned mussels
unpeeled prawns to garnish

Cut the chicken flesh into bite-sized pieces. Heat the oil in a deep frying pan or paella pan and add the chicken, pork and sausage. Sauté for 5 minutes over a high heat. Add the onion and continue to cook, over a low heat, for 5 minutes, stirring from time to time. Stir in the tomatoes and cook for 3 minutes then add the rice. Cook, stirring continuously, for a further 5 minutes. Add the peas, red pepper, seasoning and saffron or turmeric. Stir well and add the stock. Bring to the boil, cover and simmer for about 20 minutes until all the liquid has been absorbed and the rice is tender. Stir from time to time during the cooking.

Place in an ovenproof dish and stir in the parsley, prawns and mussels. Cover and cook in a moderate oven (160°C, 325°F, Gas Mark 3) for 5–10 minutes. Serve garnished with unpeeled prawns.

Risotto with leeks and bacon

SERVES 4

450 g/1 lb streaky bacon, rind removed and
chopped
4 tablespoons oil
4 leeks, chopped
450 g/1 lb long-grain rice
1 (396-g/14-oz) can peeled tomatoes
salt and freshly ground black pepper
½ teaspoon cayenne pepper
½ teaspoon ground cumin
1 teaspoon grated lemon rind
900 ml/1½ pints chicken stock
15 g/½ oz butter
grated Parmesan cheese (optional)

Fry the bacon in a large saucepan for about 8 minutes,
or until crisp and golden. Remove with a slotted spoon
and set aside. Add the oil to the bacon fat and fry the
leeks for about 12 minutes. Stir in the rice and fry for
5 minutes, stirring frequently. Add the tomatoes with
their can juice, seasoning to taste, the cayenne, cumin,
lemon rind and stock and bring to the boil.

Return the chopped bacon to the pan, cover and simmer for 15–20 minutes, or until the rice is cooked and has
absorbed all of the liquid. Serve at once dotted with
the butter and sprinkle with the cheese, if used.

French lamb casserole

SERVES 4

50 g/2 oz butter or margarine
2 onions, quartered
675 g/1½ lb lean stewing lamb, cut into serving-
sized pieces
40 g/1½ oz seasoned flour
600 ml/1 pint stock
salt and freshly ground black pepper
3 tablespoons tomato purée
1 clove garlic, crushed
1 bouquet garni
8 small button onions
100 g/4 oz shelled peas

Melt half the butter or margarine in a flameproof
casserole and add the onion quarters. Fry gently until
golden, about 8 minutes. Add the meat and fry gently
until brown on all sides, about 10 minutes. Shower in
the flour and cook for 1 minute. Gradually blend in
the stock and season to taste. Add the tomato purée,
garlic and bouquet garni. Cover and cook in a moderate
oven (180°C, 350°F, Gas Mark 4) for 1¼ hours, or until
the meat is tender.

Meanwhile, cook the button onions in the remaining
butter or margarine until golden, about 8 minutes. Add
to the casserole with the peas and cook for a further
20 minutes.

Stuffed breast of veal

———— SERVES 4–6 ————

1 (1.4–1.8-kg/3–4-lb) breast of veal or lamb
2 teaspoons lemon juice
salt and freshly ground black pepper
flour to dust
25 g/1 oz butter or margarine
2 tablespoons olive oil
STUFFING
25 g/1 oz butter or margarine
1 small onion, chopped
225 g/8 oz pork sausagemeat
1 tablespoon chopped parsley
1 egg, beaten
225 g/8 oz frozen chopped spinach, defrosted

Sprinkle the veal or lamb with the lemon juice and season generously.

Prepare the stuffing by melting the butter in a small saucepan. Add the onion and cook for 5 minutes. Mix the onion with the sausagemeat, parsley, egg, spinach and seasoning to taste. Lay this stuffing down the centre of the veal or lamb. Form into a neat roll and tie up with fine string. Dust with a little flour and place in a roasting tin. Dot with the butter and pour over the oil. Roast in a moderate oven (180°C, 350°F, Gas Mark 4) for 1½–2 hours, basting frequently. Serve sliced.

Kidney and sausage ragoût

———— SERVES 4 ————

2 tablespoons oil
350 g/12 oz lamb's kidneys, cored and halved
225 g/8 oz chipolata sausages
100 g/4 oz carrots, thinly sliced
1 medium onion, thinly sliced
2 tablespoons flour
300 ml/½ pint stock
2 tablespoons brandy (optional)
1 tablespoon tomato purée
salt and freshly ground black pepper
1 large green pepper, deseeded and chopped
2 bay leaves

Heat the oil in a medium-sized flameproof casserole and brown the kidneys on all sides. Remove with a slotted spoon and set aside. Add the sausages to the pan juices and brown on all sides. Remove and slice each chipolata diagonally.

Add the carrot and onion to the remaining pan juices and cook until golden brown. Stir in the flour, stock, brandy if used, tomato purée and seasoning to taste. Bring to the boil.

Return the kidneys and sausages to the pan. Add the green pepper and bay leaves. Cover and cook in a cool oven (150°C, 300°F, Gas Mark 2) for about 40–45 minutes. Remove the bay leaves and serve with boiled rice and seasonal vegetables.

Lamb cobbler

675 g/1½ lb boneless lean stewing lamb, cubed
seasoned flour to coat
2 tablespoons oil
1 large onion, chopped
2 carrots, diced
1 stalk celery, chopped
450 ml/¾ pint stock
1 tablespoon tomato purée
½ teaspoon finely chopped fresh or dried
rosemary
COBBLER
225 g/8 oz self-raising flour
pinch of salt
50 g/2 oz butter or margarine
½ teaspoon dried or 1 teaspoon finely
chopped fresh rosemary
about 6 tablespoons milk
milk to glaze

Toss the lamb in seasoned flour and set aside. Heat the oil in a frying pan and cook the onion, carrot and celery over a low heat until beginning to soften, about 3–5 minutes. Remove with a slotted spoon and place in a 1.75-litre/3-pint casserole dish. Add the meat to the pan juices and brown on all sides. Transfer to the casserole.

Pour the stock into the pan juices and bring to the boil. Pour over the meat and vegetables in the casserole. Stir in the tomato purée and rosemary. Cover and cook in a moderate oven (180°C, 350°F, Gas Mark 4) for 1 hour.

Meanwhile make the cobbler topping. Sift the flour and salt into a bowl. Rub the butter or margarine into the flour mixture until it resembles fine breadcrumbs. Stir in the rosemary and mix to a soft but workable dough with the milk.

Roll out the dough on a lightly floured surface to about 2 cm/¾ inch thick. Cut into rounds using a 5-cm/2-inch plain or fluted scone cutter. Place on a greased baking tray and glaze with milk. Bake in a hot oven (220°C, 425°F, Gas Mark 7) for 15 minutes until well risen and golden brown. Place on top of the casserole and cook for a further 5 minutes. Serve at once.

Cook's Tip

This tasty lamb casserole can be finished with a variety of toppings:
French bread: Top with rounds of French bread spread with butter or a mixture of butter and herbs, butter and crushed garlic or butter and yeast extract. Cook, uncovered, for a further 15-20 minutes.
Choux buns: Top with small cooked savoury choux buns made with either cheesy or herby choux paste (see page 28). Bake in a moderately hot oven (200°C, 400°F, Gas Mark 6) for about 25 minutes.
Puff pastry shapes: Top with cut-out shapes of cooked puff pastry.

Orange-glazed leg of lamb

1 (2-kg/4½-lb) leg of lamb, boned
orange slices to garnish
STUFFING
25 g/1 oz butter
1 large onion, chopped
75 g/3 oz fresh white breadcrumbs
50 g/2 oz sultanas
50 g/2 oz seedless raisins
50 g/2 oz currants
finely grated rind of 2 oranges
½ teaspoon dried rosemary
½ teaspoon dried thyme
salt and freshly ground black pepper
juice of 1 orange
GLAZE
50 g/2 oz soft brown sugar
juice of ½ lemon
juice of 1 orange
2 tablespoons Worcestershire sauce
SAUCE
100 ml/4 fl oz red wine
300 ml/½ pint stock

First prepare the stuffing by melting the butter in a small saucepan. Add the onion and fry until soft, about 5 minutes. Place in a bowl with the breadcrumbs, sultanas, raisins and currants. Blend in the orange rind, rosemary, thyme and seasoning to taste. Bind together with the orange juice.

Pack the stuffing into the lamb and then tie the joint into a neat shape with string. Place in a roasting tin.

Place all the glaze ingredients in a small saucepan and cook over a low heat for 1 minute then spoon over the meat. Roast in a moderately hot oven (190°C, 375°F, Gas Mark 5) for 2 hours, basting frequently, until cooked.

Remove the joint to a heated serving dish and keep warm. Stir the wine and stock for the sauce into the pan juices and reduce over a high heat until the sauce has thickened and all the meat residue is incorporated.

Remove the string from the meat and serve sliced with the sauce, garnished with orange slices.

Variation

Three-fruit glazed leg of lamb
Substitute the juice of 1 orange in the above recipe for 3 tablespoons grapefruit juice and 3 tablespoons orange juice for a lemon, orange and grapefruit glaze.

Osso buco

— SERVES 4 —

675–900 g/1½–2 lb knuckle of veal
25 g/1 oz seasoned flour
25 g/1 oz butter or margarine
3 onions, sliced
3 carrots, sliced
3 tomatoes, peeled and sliced
1 stalk celery, chopped
1 bouquet garni
salt and freshly ground black pepper
grated rind and juice of 1 lemon
300 ml/½ pint white wine or stock
1 tablespoon tomato purée
dash of Tabasco sauce
chopped parsley to garnish

Cut the meat into fairly large, neat pieces and roll in the seasoned flour. Heat the butter or margarine in a flameproof casserole and cook the onion for 5 minutes. Add the meat, carrot, tomatoes, celery, bouquet garni and seasoning to taste. Cook for 2–3 minutes. Stir in the lemon rind, lemon juice, white wine or stock, tomato purée and Tabasco. Cover and simmer for 2 hours.

When the veal is cooked, lift the meat into a warmed serving dish. Rub the sauce through a sieve and pour over the meat. Garnish with chopped parsley and serve with rice.

Veal goulash with herby dumplings

— SERVES 4 —

675 g/1½ lb stewing veal
40 g/1½ oz lard
3 medium onions, thinly sliced
225 g/8 oz carrots, thinly sliced
2 tablespoons paprika pepper
1 tablespoon flour
450 ml/¾ pint chicken stock
2 tablespoons dry white wine
salt and freshly ground black pepper
DUMPLINGS
100 g/4 oz self-raising flour
50 g/2 oz shredded beef suet
1 teaspoon dried mixed herbs
1 teaspoon caraway seeds
6 tablespoons soured cream
2 tablespoons water
caraway seeds to sprinkle

Cut the veal into bite-sized pieces. Heat the lard in a frying pan and brown the veal on all sides. Transfer to a 1.75-litre/3-pint ovenproof dish. Lightly brown the onion and carrot in the fat and add to the dish. Sprinkle the paprika and flour into the pan juices and fry for 2–3 minutes. Gradually add the stock, wine and seasoning to taste. Pour over the veal, cover tightly and cook in a cool oven (150°C, 300°F, Gas Mark 2) for 2 hours.

Meanwhile make the dumplings by mixing the flour, suet, herbs and caraway seeds together. Bind with the soured cream and water, adding a little extra water if necessary. Divide into 16 portions, roll into dumplings and place on the goulash. Sprinkle with a few extra caraway seeds and continue to cook, uncovered, for a further 45 minutes.

Poached whiting
in piquant parsley sauce

SERVES 4

4 whiting fillets
2 (150-g/5.3-oz) cartons natural yogurt
2 teaspoons prepared mustard
4 teaspoons lemon juice
salt and freshly ground black or white pepper
4 tablespoons finely chopped parsley
lemon slices to garnish

Poach the whiting in a little water or stock until tender, about 8–10 minutes.

Meanwhile, mix together the yogurt, mustard and lemon juice in a small bowl. Heat over a saucepan of hot water until hot, but do *not* allow to boil. Season to taste and stir in the chopped parsley.

Place the cooked fish on a warmed serving dish. Spoon over the sauce and garnish with halved lemon slices.

Variation

Poached whiting in cool mint sauce
Substitute the parsley in the above recipe with 4 table-spoons finely-chopped fresh mint leaves for a deliciously different yet calorie-conscious fish sauce.

Honey-stuffed
baked mackerel

SERVES 4

4 small mackerel, gutted and cleaned
50 g/2 oz fresh white breadcrumbs
50 g/2 oz dried apricots, chopped
1 teaspoon dried tarragon
4 teaspoons clear honey
salt and freshly ground black pepper
150 ml/¼ pint dry white wine
50 g/2 oz butter
1 tablespoon chopped parsley
2 tablespoons double cream

Grease a large ovenproof dish. Slit down the belly of each gutted fish and press down on a board, skin side up, with the palm of the hand to remove the backbone. Turn the fish over, remove the backbone and any other small bones present.

Mix the breadcrumbs, apricots and tarragon together. Stir in the honey and season to taste. If necessary, add a little extra honey to bind. Divide the stuffing into four portions and use to stuff the fish cavities. Place in the dish, pour over the wine, dot with the butter and cover with aluminium cooking foil. Cook in a moderate oven (180°C, 350°F, Gas Mark 4) for 35 minutes. Remove the foil and transfer the fish to a warmed serving dish. Stir the parsley and cream into the sauce and serve poured over the fish.

47

Pasta and pepper casserole

SERVES 6

900 g/2 lb stewing steak
2 medium onions, chopped
50 g/2 oz lard
2 teaspoons ground ginger
2 teaspoons soy sauce
1.15 litres/2 pints beef stock
4 tablespoons chopped parsley
salt and freshly ground black pepper
grated rind of 1 large lemon
350 g/12 oz pasta bows or rigatoni
1 (400-g/14-oz) can sweet red peppers, drained and sliced
chopped parsley to garnish

Cut the stewing steak into bite-sized pieces. Cook the onion in the lard with the steak until browned on all sides, and place in a large flameproof casserole. Add the ginger, soy sauce, beef stock and parsley. Season generously and bring to the boil. Reduce the heat and simmer gently for about 1½ hours until the meat is tender.

Add the lemon rind, pasta and peppers. Cook gently for a further 15 minutes until the pasta is tender and the excess liquid has been absorbed. Adjust the seasoning if necessary before serving sprinkled with parsley.

Fish boulangère

SERVES 4

50 g/2 oz butter
1 clove garlic, crushed
675 g/1½ lb white fish fillets (cod, haddock or plaice for example), skinned and cut into bite-sized pieces
salt and freshly ground black pepper
1 large onion, sliced into rings
2 tablespoons chopped parsley
450 g/1 lb potatoes, par-cooked and thinly sliced

Mix half the butter with the garlic and spread on the base of a 1.25-litre/2-pint ovenproof dish. Cover with the pieces of fish. Season lightly, top with the onion and sprinkle with the parsley. Place the potato slices on top in an overlapping pattern. Dot with the remaining butter and bake in a moderate oven (180°C, 350°F, Gas Mark 4) for 45 minutes, until the potato topping is crisp and golden and the fish is cooked.

Variation

For those who are counting the calories the potato topping in the above recipe can be replaced with slices of courgettes. Slice 450 g/1 lb courgettes and place on top of the fish mixture in an overlapping pattern. Dot with the remaining butter and bake in a moderate oven (180°C, 350°F, Gas Mark 4) for 30 minutes.

Coley crumble

— SERVES 4 —

675 g/1½ lb coley fillet, skinned and cut into
bite-sized pieces
3 tablespoons oil
1 tablespoon vinegar
1 large Spanish onion, chopped
salt and freshly ground black pepper
100 g/4 oz plain flour
50 g/2 oz butter or margarine
50 g/2 oz Cheddar cheese, grated
1 (425-g/15-oz) can peeled tomatoes, drained

Place the coley in a 1.25-litre/2-pint ovenproof dish.
Mix the oil, vinegar, onion and seasoning to taste
together and pour over the fish. Leave to marinate for
30 minutes.

Meanwhile sift the flour into a bowl, add a pinch of
salt and rub in the butter or margarine. Stir in the
cheese. Place the tomatoes on top of the fish and sprinkle
with the cheese crumble. Bake in a moderately hot oven
(190°C, 375°F, Gas Mark 5) for 30 minutes or until
golden. Serve hot.

Corsican veal cutlets

— SERVES 4 —

4 veal cutlets
salt and freshly ground black pepper
25 g/1 oz butter or margarine
1 onion stock cube, crumbled
2 tomatoes, peeled and sliced
2 teaspoons dried basil
1 small green pepper, deseeded, sliced and
blanched
40 g/1½ oz Cheddar cheese, grated

Place the cutlets on a grill pan and season well. Dot
with the butter or margarine and cook under a moderate
grill for about 10 minutes. Turn over, sprinkle with the
crumbled stock cube and cook for a further 10 minutes.

Cover with the sliced tomatoes, basil, pepper and
cheese. Grill for a further 5 minutes or until the cheese
has melted. Serve hot.

Cook's Tip

To peel tomatoes simply plunge into a bowl of boiling
water for 45 seconds. Remove with a slotted spoon and
peel away the now loose skin.

Barbecued spareribs

2 tablespoons oil
1 clove garlic, crushed
1 large onion, finely chopped
1 (141-g/5-oz) can tomato purée
3 tablespoons lemon juice
$\frac{1}{2}$ teaspoon salt
$\frac{1}{4}$ teaspoon freshly ground black pepper
$\frac{1}{2}$ teaspoon dried sage
4 tablespoons light brown sugar
100 ml/4 fl oz beef stock
4 tablespoons Worcestershire sauce
2 teaspoons dry mustard powder
1.4 kg/3 lb pork spareribs
spring onions to garnish

Heat the oil in a large frying pan. When hot sauté the garlic and onion for 2–3 minutes until soft but not brown. Add the tomato purée, lemon juice, salt, pepper, sage, sugar, beef stock, Worcestershire sauce and mustard. Stir well to combine. Heat until boiling.

Meanwhile, cut the spareribs into serving-sized pieces. Place on a rack in a large roasting tin. Spoon the boiling sauce evenly over the spareribs. Bake in a moderately hot oven (200°C, 400°F, Gas Mark 6) for 1 hour, or until the spareribs are brown and crisp. Baste the ribs with the sauce from time to time during cooking. Serve the spareribs hot with any extra sauce and garnish with spring onions.

Cook's Tip

Chinese barbecued spareribs and Sweet 'n' sour meatballs look all the more authentic if they are presented with traditional vegetable garnishes:
Curled spring onions: Trim the green tops off the spring onions, thinly slice any remaining green lengthways to the bulb. Chill in iced water to curl.
Celery curls: Cut sticks of celery into pieces 7.5 cm/3 inches long. Slit each piece into narrow strips, almost to the end. Chill in iced water until the ends curl.
Vegetable shapes: Thinly slice a peeled turnip, carrot or swede crossways and cut out shapes with canapé cutters or with a sharp knife. Traditional shapes include birds, fish and the moon.

Sweet 'n' sour meatballs

1 medium onion, finely chopped
25 g/1 oz butter or margarine
450 g/1 lb minced beef
50 g/2 oz fresh white or brown breadcrumbs
1 teaspoon Worcestershire sauce
1 egg, beaten
salt and freshly ground black pepper
1 tablespoon oil
1 medium red pepper, deseeded and chopped
1 medium green pepper, deseeded and chopped
2 tablespoons soft brown sugar
2 teaspoons soy sauce
2 tablespoons vinegar
150 ml/$\frac{1}{4}$ pint unsweetened orange juice
150 ml/$\frac{1}{4}$ pint beef stock
1 tablespoon cornflour

Cook the onion in the butter or margarine, in a small saucepan, until soft but not brown. Add the cooked onion to the minced beef with the breadcrumbs, Worcestershire sauce and egg. Mix well and season generously.

Using damp hands, shape the mixture into 12 large meatballs. Heat the oil in a frying pan and cook the meatballs over a high heat until browned on all sides. Remove with a slotted spoon and place in a 1.25-litre/ 2-pint covered casserole dish. Add the peppers to the frying pan and sauté for 2 minutes until beginning to soften. Stir in the sugar, soy sauce, vinegar, orange juice and stock. Bring to the boil then pour over the meatballs.

Cover and cook in a moderate oven (180°C, 350°F, Gas Mark 4) for 45 minutes. Strain the cooking stock into a small saucepan. Add the cornflour, dissolved in a little water, and bring the mixture to the boil. Cook for 2 minutes then pour over the meatballs. Serve with boiled rice, buttered noodles or jacket potatoes.

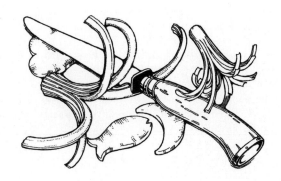

Chicken provençal

— SERVES 4 —

4 tablespoons oil
4 chicken portions
2 onions, chopped
2 cloves garlic, crushed
2 green peppers, deseeded and finely diced
300 ml/½ pint dry white wine or stock
6 tomatoes, peeled and chopped
1 tablespoon tomato purée
1 bay leaf
1 teaspoon dried oregano
salt and freshly ground black pepper

Heat the oil in a flameproof casserole and fry the chicken on all sides until golden. Remove with a slotted spoon and add the onion, garlic and peppers. Cook for about 5 minutes to soften then drain away any excess oil. Return the chicken to the casserole. Add the wine, tomatoes, tomato purée, bay leaf and oregano. Season generously then cover and simmer for 1¼ hours.

Remove the bay leaf and adjust the seasoning before serving with saffron rice.

Smoked mackerel gougère

— SERVES 4 —

350 g/12 oz smoked mackerel fillets
1 medium onion, sliced
150 g/5 oz butter
175 g/6 oz plain flour
300 ml/½ pint milk
3 tablespoons cider
2 tablespoons natural yogurt
salt and freshly ground white pepper
300 ml/½ pint water
4 eggs, beaten
75 g/3 oz Cheddar cheese, grated
1 tablespoon dried breadcrumbs
chopped chives or parsley to garnish

Skin the mackerel fillets and flake the flesh. Fry the onion in a heavy-based pan in 25 g/1 oz of the butter until soft and golden. Add 25 g/1 oz of the flour and stir well to mix. Gradually add the milk and bring to the boil. Boil for 1 minute then remove from the heat. Stir in the cider, yogurt, flaked fish and seasoning to taste.

Meanwhile make the choux pastry for the gougère. Melt the remaining butter in a saucepan with the water. Bring to the boil, take off the heat and beat in the remaining flour until just smooth. Beat in the eggs, a little at a time, then finally beat in the cheese.

Spoon the choux pastry around the sides of a 1.25-litre/2-pint shallow ovenproof dish. Spoon the fish sauce into the centre, sprinkle with the breadcrumbs and bake in a moderately hot oven (200°C, 400°F, Gas Mark 6) for 40–45 minutes. Serve garnished with chives or parsley.

Sweet'n'sour pork

SERVES 4–6

900 g/2 lb lean pork, cut into 2-cm/¾-inch cubes
2 teaspoons salt
2 tablespoons cornflour
8 tablespoons self-raising flour
150 ml/¼ pint water
2 eggs, beaten
oil for deep frying
SAUCE
1 tablespoon oil
1 large green pepper, deseeded and sliced
1 large red pepper, deseeded and sliced
1 onion, chopped
25 g/1 oz fresh root ginger, very finely chopped
1 carrot, very thinly sliced
3 tablespoons cornflour
150 ml/¼ pint water
6 tablespoons wine vinegar
5 tablespoons dark brown sugar
6 tablespoons tangerine or orange juice
4 tablespoons dry sherry
3 tablespoons soy sauce
4 tablespoons tomato purée

Rub the pork with the salt and dust in the cornflour. Mix the flour, water and eggs together. Coat the pork with this batter mixture. Heat the oil to 180°C/350°F, or until a cube of day-old bread turns golden in 1 minute. Deep fry the pieces of pork for about 5 minutes, until golden brown. Drain.

Meanwhile make the sauce by heating the oil in a large frying pan. Add the peppers, onion, root ginger and carrot. Stir fry for 2 minutes. Mix the remaining sauce ingredients together and pour into the mixture. Stir until the sauce thickens and clears. Serve the pork with the sauce poured over.

Soured cream pot-roast

SERVES 6

1 (1.4-kg/3-lb) middle/end of forehock bacon
joint
600 ml/1 pint stock
grated rind of 1 lemon
1 bay leaf
225 g/8 oz small carrots
225 g/8 oz small button onions
100 g/4 oz button mushrooms
300 ml/½ pint soured cream
2 tablespoons cornflour
salt and freshly ground black pepper

Place the bacon joint in a large saucepan and cover with cold water. Bring to the boil and simmer for 30 minutes. Drain and discard the cooking water and add the stock, lemon rind, bay leaf, carrots and onions. Bring to the boil then cover and simmer for a further 30 minutes.

Add the mushrooms, soured cream, cornflour blended with a little water and seasoning to taste. Cover and simmer for a further 20 minutes.

Serve the bacon joint sliced on a serving dish surrounded with the cooked vegetables. Serve any extra sauce separately in a sauce boat.

Somerset beef casserole

— SERVES 4 —

675 g/1½ lb stewing beef, cubed
25 g/1 oz seasoned flour
25 g/1 oz butter or margarine
3 medium onions, sliced
4 stalks celery, chopped
300 ml/½ pint dry cider
300 ml/½ pint beef stock
1 tablespoon black treacle
1 large cooking apple, peeled, cored and sliced
225 g/8 oz frozen sweetcorn with peppers, defrosted
1 teaspoon dried rosemary
1 red dessert apple, sliced to garnish
DUMPLINGS
100 g/4 oz self-raising flour
1 onion stock cube, crumbled
50 g/2 oz shredded beef suet
salt and freshly ground black pepper

Coat the meat in the seasoned flour. Melt the butter or margarine in a frying pan and sauté the meat for about 10 minutes or until brown on all sides. Remove with a slotted spoon and place in a 1.75-litre/3-pint casserole dish. Add the onion and celery to the pan juices and cook until browned. Stir in any remaining flour. Cook for 1 minute. Add the cider, stock, treacle, apple, sweetcorn and rosemary. Pour over the meat. Cover and cook in a moderate oven (160°C, 325°F, Gas Mark 3) for 1¾ hours. Increase the oven temperature to hot (220°C, 425°F, Gas Mark 7). Prepare the dumplings. Mix the flour with the onion cube, suet and seasoning. Bind with sufficient cold water to make a soft dough. Shape into nine dumplings. Place on top of the meat and bake for 20 minutes. Garnish with halved apple slices.

Pork and pineapple curry

— SERVES 4 —

40 g/1½ oz butter or margarine
2 large onions, chopped
1 clove garlic, crushed
575 g/1¼ lb boneless lean pork, cubed
1 tablespoon flour
1–2 tablespoons curry powder, according to taste
4 canned pineapple rings, chopped
1 tablespoon tomato purée
150 g/2 oz seedless raisins
1 tablespoon lemon juice
1 bay leaf
1 teaspoon ground ginger
1 teaspoon salt
300 ml/½ pint stock
150 ml/¼ pint milk

Heat the butter or margarine in a saucepan. Add the onion and garlic and fry until soft, about 5 minutes. Add the pork and fry quickly to brown on all sides. Stir in the flour and curry powder. Add the remaining ingredients and bring to the boil, stirring continuously. Reduce the heat, cover and simmer for 2 hours, or until the pork is tender. Stir from time to time to prevent sticking.

Serve the curry with boiled rice, desiccated coconut and chutney.

Spaghetti
with bacon sauce

—— SERVES 6 ——

3 tablespoons oil
2 medium onions, sliced
1 clove garlic, crushed
675 g/1½ lb lean collar bacon, rind removed and
very finely chopped
2 tablespoons flour
3 tablespoons tomato purée
2 teaspoons dried sage
450 g/1 lb tomatoes, peeled, deseeded and
quartered
3 tablespoons dry white wine
450 ml/¾ pint unseasoned stock
freshly ground black pepper
350 g/12 oz spaghetti
salt
25 g/1 oz butter, melted
grated Parmesan cheese to serve

Heat the oil in a large heavy-based saucepan. Add the
onion and cook until golden brown. Add the garlic and
cook for a further 1 minute. Stir in the bacon and sauté,
stirring, for about 5 minutes. Sprinkle over the flour
and cook for 1 minute. Gradually add the tomato purée,
sage, tomatoes, wine and stock to make a thin sauce.
Season with pepper then cook, uncovered, for about
50 minutes or until the mixture is reduced by about
half and the sauce has thickened.

Meanwhile, just before the sauce is cooked, cook the
spaghetti in boiling salted water until just tender,
about 10–12 minutes. Drain well and toss in the melted
butter.

Serve the spaghetti with the bacon sauce and sprinkled
with Parmesan cheese to taste.

Roast beef
and Yorkshire pudding

—— SERVES 6–8 ——

1 (1.6–1.8-kg/3½–4-lb) joint of roasting beef
2 tablespoons dripping
salt and freshly ground black pepper
YORKSHIRE PUDDING
1 quantity pancake batter *(see Vegetable pancakes,
page 62)*
GRAVY
1 tablespoon flour
300 ml/½ pint stock

Place the beef in a roasting tin and dot with the dripping.
Season to taste and bake in a hot oven (220°C, 425°F,
Gas Mark 7) for 15 minutes. Reduce the oven temperature
to moderately hot (190°C, 375°F, Gas Mark 5) and continue to roast for a further 15 minutes per 450 g/1 lb
for rare beef, or 20 minutes per 450 g/1 lb for medium to
well done beef.

Make the batter for the Yorkshire pudding according
to the recipe instructions, substituting ½ teaspoon salt
for a pinch of salt.

Remove the beef from the oven when cooked and keep
warm. Increase the oven temperature to 230°C, 450°F,
Gas Mark 8. Cover the bottom of a baking tin with a
thin layer of fat from the roast, heat in the oven until
smoking hot and pour in the batter. Bake on the top
shelf of the oven for 25 minutes until well risen, crisp
and golden brown. The puddings can be made in small
bun tins and cooked for 15 minutes.

Meanwhile make the gravy. Pour off almost all the fat
from the roasting tin but retain the meat juices. Mix the
flour into the meat juices and cook for 1 minute. Gradually add the stock and bring to the boil to make a smooth
gravy. Serve the beef sliced with Yorkshire pudding and
gravy, and accompany with seasonal vegetables.

Salads and Vegetables

Piquant, crunchy and colourful—get the mix right, and a salad can make a stunning meal. Coupled with ideas using honest-to-goodness vegetables packed with nourishment, you will have an unfailing back-up in this chapter of original main dishes with a difference.

If you thought salads simply consisted of the same old greenery then you're in for a few surprises. The fact is salads have no season or strict culinary boundary. Start simply with crisp greens in season, then add the attraction of meat, fish, eggs, cheese or fruit to provide a variety of different flavours. Topped or tossed with a whole host of dressings from piquant French to creamy mayonnaise there can be a different surprise in every mouthful.

Wholesome vegetables provide a dependable accompaniment to a great many main dishes and sauces, yet served without meat they also give a cheap, yet flavoursome, alternative family meal. Flans, casseroles, ragoûts, soufflés, escalops and fritters made with vegetables are among the inexpensive and sustaining variations possible and they are packed with great nutritional value. Meat could be added to many of the following recipes but they are just as delicious without.

Salad niçoise; Wurst salad
(see overleaf)

Salad niçoise

1 firm lettuce heart, washed
225 g/8 oz French beans, cooked
1 onion, cut into rings
1 (198-g/7-oz) can tuna fish, flaked
8 black olives, stoned
1 (50-g/1¾-oz) can anchovy fillets, drained
4 ripe tomatoes, quartered
2 hard-boiled eggs, quartered
1 tablespoon chopped parsley
vinaigrette dressing to serve

Arrange the lettuce, broken into bite-sized pieces, in the base of a salad bowl. Cut the cooked beans into short lengths and arrange over the lettuce with the onion, tuna fish, black olives, anchovy fillets and tomatoes.

Top with the hard-boiled egg quarters and sprinkle with chopped parsley.

Just before serving pour over vinaigrette dressing to taste and serve with crusty French bread.

Cook's Tip

You can make a good vinaigrette dressing by mixing ¾ teaspoon salt, ¼ teaspoon pepper, ¾ teaspoon dry mustard powder with ¾ teaspoon sugar in a bowl. Add 4 tablespoons vinegar and stir well until the sugar has dissolved. Gradually beat in 8 tablespoons olive or vegetable oil to make a thick creamy dressing.

Wurst salad

450 g/1 lb mixed cooked German wurst, sliced
1 medium green pepper, deseeded and sliced
1 medium red pepper, deseeded and sliced
1 small onion, thinly sliced into rings
100 ml/4 fl oz French dressing
2 small pickled gherkins

Arrange the sliced wurst and peppers decoratively on a serving dish. Scatter over the onion rings and pour over the French dressing. Thinly slice the gherkins lengthways, leaving each slice attached at the top. Open out into fans and use to garnish the salad. Chill slightly before serving with crusty warm bread.

Cook's Tip

The Germans say that they produce almost 1500 different sausages so there is quite a variety to choose from. Consider the following—they can all be served cold in a salad:

Bierschinken: This is a large sausage distinguishable by small chunks of cooked ham fat and sometimes pistachio nuts.

Bierwurst: A spicy sausage made from roughly-chopped pork and sometimes flavoured with garlic.

Fleischwurst: A juicy, hearty-flavoured sausage of finely-chopped meat that is pink to light brown in colour and flavoured with garlic.

German cervelat: A smoked sausage made of finely-minced beef and pork with a characteristic golden brown casing and pink flesh.

Katenrauchwurst: A black-skinned sausage containing pieces of smoked pork that is coarse but firm in texture.

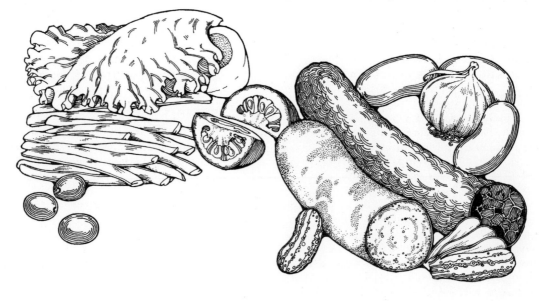

Greek salad

SERVES 4

1 Cos lettuce
1 bunch of radishes, sliced
225 g/8 oz feta cheese, cubed
large pinch of dried marjoram
4 tomatoes, peeled and sliced
6 anchovy fillets, finely chopped
6 large black olives, halved and stoned
1 tablespoon finely chopped parsley
$\frac{1}{2}$ teaspoon freshly ground black pepper
DRESSING
4 tablespoons olive oil
4 teaspoons white wine vinegar
1 tablespoon finely chopped fresh mixed herbs
4 spring onions, chopped
1 teaspoon sugar
pinch of salt

Tear the lettuce into bite-sized pieces and arrange on a large serving dish. Scatter the radish slices over the top. Pile the cheese in the centre of the dish and sprinkle with the marjoram. Place the tomatoes in a circle around the cheese and place the anchovies on top of the tomatoes, alternating with the black olives. Sprinkle with the parsley and the black pepper.

Mix the dressing ingredients together in a screw-topped jar and pour over the salad just before serving.

Provençal seafood salad

SERVES 6

1 Cos or Webb lettuce, washed and separated
into leaves
300 ml/$\frac{1}{2}$ pint thick mayonnaise
1 clove garlic, finely chopped
2 anchovy fillets, finely chopped
1 tablespoon finely chopped fresh basil or
tarragon
2 tablespoons finely chopped parsley
1 tablespoon finely chopped capers
2 teaspoons lemon juice
450 g/1 lb cooked white fish, diced
100 g/4 oz unpeeled prawns
3–4 tomatoes, peeled and quartered
4–6 black olives, stoned and halved
French dressing to serve

Line a salad bowl with the lettuce and chill. Combine the mayonnaise, garlic, anchovies, herbs, capers and lemon juice in a bowl. Toss the fish lightly in this mixture and pile into the centre of the salad bowl.

Garnish the salad with the prawns, tomatoes and black olives. Serve with a little French dressing poured over.

Ox tongue and orange salad

— SERVES 4 —

450 g/1 lb cooked ox tongue, cubed
½ teaspoon salt
¼ teaspoon freshly ground black pepper
4 tablespoons olive oil
4 tablespoons fresh orange juice
1 tablespoon finely grated lemon rind
4 tablespoons lemon juice
1 tablespoon capers
6 oranges, peeled, pith removed and segmented
2 heads of chicory

Place the tongue in a mixing bowl with the salt, pepper and 1 tablespoon of the oil. Mix well.

Place the remaining oil, the orange juice, lemon rind, lemon juice and capers in a screw-topped jar. Shake vigorously then pour over the tongue. Add the orange segments and toss to mix.

Divide the chicory into leaves and wash well. Line the edge of a serving dish with the chicory leaves and pile the tongue mixture into the centre. Serve at once.

Chicken Waldorf Salad

— SERVES 4–6 —

1 (1.4-kg/3-lb) chicken, roasted
3 sticks celery, finely chopped
4 medium dessert apples, cored and diced
150 ml/¼ pint mayonnaise
150 ml/¼ pint single or soured cream
lemon juice
40–50 g/1½–2 oz walnut halves, coarsely chopped
1 crisp lettuce heart
watercress sprigs to garnish

Remove the flesh from the cooked chicken carcass and dice into bite-sized pieces. In a mixing bowl combine the chicken, celery and apple.

Blend the mayonnaise with the single or soured cream and sharpen to taste with lemon juice. Fold the mayonnaise through the chicken mixture and chill until ready to serve.

Just before serving fold the chopped walnuts through the chicken salad mixture. Arrange the lettuce leaves over the base of a serving dish. Spoon the chicken mixture on top and garnish with watercress sprigs. This salad is delicious served with hot herb bread.

Piquant egg salad

SERVES 4

1 head of celery, finely sliced
8 hard-boiled eggs, sliced
4 carrots, grated
2 radishes, sliced
$\frac{1}{4}$ cucumber, sliced

DRESSING

300 ml/$\frac{1}{2}$ pint natural yogurt
1 teaspoon paprika pepper
1 teaspoon sugar
1 tablespoon lemon juice
1 tablespoon orange juice
freshly ground black pepper
1 tablespoon chopped parsley

First prepare the dressing by mixing all the dressing ingredients together in a small bowl. Place the celery in another bowl and add half of the prepared dressing. Toss to coat. Spoon into a salad bowl and top with the sliced eggs. Cover with the carrot and garnish with the radishes and cucumber.

Spoon the remaining yogurt dressing over the top, chill and serve with hot French bread.

Stuffed aubergines

SERVES 4–6

3 large aubergines, halved lengthways
salt
25 g/1 oz fresh white breadcrumbs
2 tablespoons chopped parsley
1 teaspoon dried oregano
6 anchovy fillets, chopped
12 large black olives, halved, stoned and chopped
3 tomatoes, peeled and chopped
4 tablespoons olive oil
watercress sprigs to garnish

Sprinkle the aubergines with the salt and leave for 30 minutes to drain. Wash and pat dry with absorbent kitchen paper. Cut the aubergine flesh from inside the aubergines and dice into chunks. Reserve the aubergine shells.

Mix the aubergine flesh with the breadcrumbs, parsley, oregano, anchovies, olives and tomatoes. Mix well to blend. Turn the mixture into the reserved aubergine shells and place in a shallow ovenproof dish. Sprinkle with the oil, cover and bake in a moderate oven (180°C, 350°F, Gas Mark 4) for 30 minutes.

Remove the cover and continue to cook for a further 20–30 minutes. Serve hot garnished with watercress sprigs.

Vegetable pancakes

PANCAKE BATTER
100 g/4 oz plain flour
pinch of salt
1 egg
1 egg yolk
300 ml/½ pint milk
2 tablespoons cold water
1 tablespoon butter, melted
oil for frying
FILLING
4 tablespoons oil
2 medium onions, finely chopped
1 small red pepper, deseeded and chopped
½ small green cabbage, shredded
1 dessert apple, peeled, cored and chopped
salt and freshly ground black pepper
1 teaspoon dried dill
25 g/1 oz butter

First make the pancakes by sifting the flour and salt into a mixing bowl. Add the egg, egg yolk and half the milk. Stir continuously to gradually draw in all the flour. Beat well to form a smooth batter. Add the remaining milk and the water and, just before using, stir in the melted butter.

Heat a 15-cm/6-inch frying pan with a little oil. Pour in enough batter to cover the surface lightly. Cook over a moderate heat until lightly browned. Turn and cook for 1 more minute. Make eight pancakes this way and keep warm.

Meanwhile prepare the filling. Heat the oil in another frying pan. Add the onion and pepper and fry for 5 minutes. Add the cabbage, apple, seasoning and dill. Cook for a further 5 minutes.

Spread each pancake with about 2 tablespoons of the vegetable mixture. Roll up to enclose the filling. Arrange in a warmed, shallow flameproof serving dish. Dot with butter and grill under a low heat for 5 minutes. Serve hot.

Chesterfield casserole

3 large carrots, thickly sliced
2 large potatoes, cut into 1-cm/½-inch dice
1 medium turnip, cut into 1-cm/½-inch dice
salt and freshly ground black pepper
4 spring onions, sliced
25 g/1 oz butter
25 g/1 oz flour
300 ml/½ pint milk
1 teaspoon prepared mustard
2 eggs, separated
75 g/3 oz Cheddar cheese, grated
GARNISH
1 tomato, sliced
parsley sprigs

Cook the carrot, potato and turnip in boiling, salted water for 10 minutes. Add the spring onions and cook for a further 5 minutes. Drain thoroughly. Season generously and place in a 1.75-litre/3-pint ovenproof dish.

Melt the butter in a saucepan. Add the flour and cook for 1 minute. Gradually stir in the milk to make a smooth sauce. Bring to the boil, season to taste and add the mustard. Remove from the heat, allow to cool slightly, then beat in the egg yolks and cheese, stirring until well blended.

Whisk the egg whites until stiff then fold into the sauce. Pour over the cooked vegetables and bake in a moderately hot oven (200°C, 400°F, Gas Mark 6) until well risen and firm, about 30–40 minutes. Serve garnished with the sliced tomato and parsley sprigs.

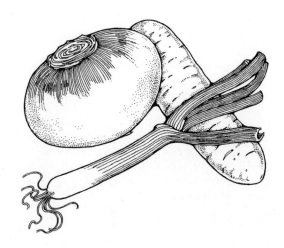

Country cabbage rolls

— SERVES 4 —

12 large cabbage leaves
225 g/8 oz pork sausagemeat
1 small onion, grated
225 g/8 oz fresh white breadcrumbs
2 hard-boiled eggs, finely chopped
100 g/4 oz button mushrooms, finely chopped
1 teaspoon dried thyme
salt and freshly ground black pepper
SAUCE
1 (396-g/14-oz) can peeled tomatoes, chopped
300 ml/½ pint hot stock
1 tablespoon dark brown sugar
1 tablespoon red wine vinegar
2 teaspoons cornflour
chopped parsley to garnish

Cut away the thick stem from each cabbage leaf. Plunge into boiling water and blanch for 1 minute. Cool in cold water and drain thoroughly.

Mix the sausagemeat, onion, breadcrumbs, eggs, mushrooms and thyme together. Season to taste. Divide the mixture into 12 portions and place one portion in the centre of each cabbage leaf. Roll up to enclose the filling. Place in a shallow ovenproof dish. Mix the tomatoes with their can juice, the stock, sugar and vinegar. Pour over the cabbage rolls.

Cover and bake in a moderately hot oven (190°C, 375°F, Gas Mark 5) for 50 minutes. When cooked lift the cabbage rolls from the tomato sauce and keep hot. Stir the cornflour, dissolved in a little water, into the sauce and cook for 2 minutes to thicken. Season to taste. Serve the cabbage rolls with the sauce poured over, garnished with chopped parsley.

Leek and potato fries

— SERVES 4 —

350 g/12 oz leeks, sliced
100 g/4 oz butter
450 g/1 lb potatoes
200 g/7 oz fresh brown breadcrumbs
2 eggs
salt and freshly ground black pepper
flour to coat
3 tablespoons lemon juice
2 tablespoons chopped parsley
3 tablespoons oil

Sauté the leeks lightly in 25 g/1 oz of the butter, and allow to cool. Meanwhile boil the potatoes, drain and mash. Allow to cool.

In a mixing bowl combine the leek, potato, breadcrumbs and eggs. Season generously. Divide into 16 portions and form each into a flat cake. Flour the cakes lightly. Chill for at least 30 minutes.

Cream 50 g/2 oz of the butter with the lemon juice and parsley. Form into a log shape and chill, wrapped in greaseproof paper.

To cook, heat the remaining butter and oil in a frying pan and fry the cakes for 2–3 minutes on each side. Serve with slices of the chilled parsley and lemon butter.

Vegetable strudels

SERVES 4–6

2 tablespoons oil
2 onions, chopped
100 g/4 oz mushrooms, chopped
2 tomatoes, peeled and chopped
350 g/12 oz frozen chopped spinach, defrosted
1 tablespoon chopped nuts
salt and freshly ground black pepper
½ teaspoon dried mixed herbs
1 tablespoon chopped parsley
1 (368-g/13-oz) packet frozen puff pastry, defrosted
4 teaspoons butter, melted
25 g/1 oz toasted dry breadcrumbs
sesame seeds to coat
GARNISH
tomato wedges
parsley sprigs

Heat the oil in a saucepan. Add the onion and fry until golden brown, about 8 minutes. Add the mushrooms, tomatoes, spinach, nuts, seasoning to taste and herbs. Cook for a further 10 minutes and leave to cool.

Roll out the pastry on a lightly floured surface to a 35-cm/14-inch square. Cut in half lengthways to make two rectangles measuring 35 × 18 cm/14 × 7 inches. Brush the pastry oblongs with one-third of the melted butter each. Sprinkle each with half the toasted bread-crumbs. Divide the filling in half and spread each to within 2.5 cm/1 inch of the edges of the pastry oblongs. Dampen the edges with water and roll both oblongs up, from the short end like Swiss rolls. Brush with the remaining melted butter and sprinkle with sesame seeds. Place on two dampened baking trays and bake in a hot oven (220°C, 425°F, Gas Mark 7) for about 30 minutes until well risen and golden. Garnish with tomato wedges and parsley sprigs.

Cheesy potato fritters

SERVES 4

900 g/2 lb potatoes
2 tablespoons chopped parsley
salt and freshly ground black pepper
100 g/4 oz Lancashire cheese, cubed
flour to coat
1 egg, beaten
dried breadcrumbs to coat
oil for deep frying

Cook the potatoes in boiling salted water for 20–30 minutes until tender. Drain well and mash with the chopped parsley. Season lightly. Using lightly floured hands, roll spoonfuls of the mixture into balls. Place a cube of cheese in the centre of each potato ball and reshape.

Coat the fritters in flour, then in beaten egg and finally roll in breadcrumbs. Heat the oil for frying to 180°C/350°F, or until a cube of day-old bread turns golden in 1 minute. Deep fry the fritters for 10–15 minutes until crisp and golden. Drain on absorbent kitchen paper and serve at once on a bed of shredded lettuce.

Cook-ahead Meals

No one wants to slave over a hot stove when outside the temperature is soaring, spend the entire evening in the kitchen when guests come for dinner or waste valuable time when family and friends have the opportunity to get together at weekends.

You needn't with the time and flavour-tested recipes in this chapter. All designed to be prepared well ahead they need little or no attention before serving. Chill or freeze away the dishes until required.

Curries and casseroles make wonderful cook-ahead meals since their preparation can be done in advance and many really improve upon second day eating. The art of making a good curry or casserole dish does not lie in any culinary wizardry but in long, slow, gentle cooking which leaves you plenty of time to deal with last-minute accompaniments and other courses. For convenience and fuel economy why not cook the recipes in bulk and store them away in the freezer for when time is at a premium?

Pies and pastry items can also prove a valuable asset to the prepare and cook-ahead enthusiast but for fresh results cook raw pastry items on the day of serving.

Sicilian savoury oranges; Chicken pockets (see overleaf)

Chicken pockets

SERVES 4

50 g/2 oz cream cheese
15 g/$\frac{1}{2}$ oz butter
$\frac{1}{2}$ clove garlic, crushed
1 teaspoon finely chopped parsley
salt and freshly ground black pepper
4 chicken breasts
25 g/1 oz seasoned flour
1 large egg, beaten
75 g/3 oz fresh white breadcrumbs
oil for deep frying

Cream the cheese and butter together in a bowl. Add the garlic, parsley and seasoning to taste. Form the mixture into a pat and wrap in greaseproof paper. Chill for 20 minutes.

Remove any bones from the chicken breasts and skin. Place each breast between two sheets of greaseproof paper and beat out until 1 cm/$\frac{1}{2}$ inch thick. Lay each chicken breast out flat. Divide the chilled cheese mixture between the breasts. Fold the edges of the breast over, then roll up tightly. Secure each with a small skewer or wooden cocktail stick.

Dip each chicken roll in seasoned flour. Coat in the egg and finally the breadcrumbs. Heat the oil to 180°C/350°F, or until a cube of day-old bread turns golden in 1 minute. Deep fry the chicken breasts until crisp and golden, about 10 minutes. Drain on absorbent kitchen paper. Remove the skewers or cocktail sticks and serve with a mixed salad.

Variation

Chicken and ham pockets
Prepare the chicken breasts as above. Top with 4 slices of cooked ham, 75 g/3 oz grated Cheddar cheese and a little fresh rosemary. Fold the edges of the breast over, then roll up tightly. Continue preparing and cooking as above.

Sicilian savoury oranges

SERVES 4

225 g/8 oz short-grain rice
50 g/2 oz Parmesan cheese, grated
2 small eggs, beaten
3 tablespoons tomato purée
salt and freshly ground black pepper
50 g/2 oz Bel Paese cheese, finely diced
50 g/2 oz garlic sausage, finely diced
50 g/2 oz fine dry breadcrumbs
oil for deep frying

Cook the rice in boiling salted water until just tender, about 15–20 minutes. Place in a bowl, add the Parmesan cheese, eggs, 1 tablespoon of the tomato purée and salt to taste. Blend thoroughly and leave until cold.

Place the Bel Paese cheese and garlic sausage in a bowl. Stir in the remaining tomato purée and seasons to taste.

To make the 'oranges', place 2 teaspoons of the cooked rice mixture into the well-floured palm of one hand and mould against the hand. Put a teaspoon of the cheese and ham mixture into the hollow, top with a little more rice and completely enclose the meat and cheese mixture. Form into balls about 4 cm/1$\frac{1}{2}$ inches wide. The mixture will make about 20 balls. Coat thickly with the breadcrumbs. Heat the oil to 180°C/350°F, or until a cube of day-old bread turns golden in 1 minute. Deep fry the rice 'oranges' until golden brown, about 5 minutes. Drain on absorbent kitchen paper.

Thatched casserole

—— SERVES 4 ——

575 g/1¼ lb spare rib pork, cubed
25 g/1 oz flour
25 g/1 oz butter or margarine
2 medium onions, sliced
2 medium cooking apples, peeled, cored and
sliced
300 ml/½ pint cider
¼ teaspoon dried sage
salt and freshly ground black pepper
6 large slices white bread, crusts removed
50 g/2 oz butter, melted
dessert apple slices to garnish

Toss the pork in the flour. Melt the butter or margarine in a large saucepan, add the onion and cook for about 3 minutes. Add the pork and cook, turning, until browned on all sides. Stir in any remaining flour. Add the apples, cider, sage and seasoning and bring to the boil, stirring. Transfer to a 2.25-litre/4-pint ovenproof dish. Cover and cook in a moderate oven (180°C, 350°F, Gas Mark 4) for 1 hour.

Cut each bread slice into four strips and arrange, overlapping and radiating from the centre of the casserole on top of the meat. Brush with the melted butter and return to the oven for about 30 minutes until the bread is crisp and golden. Garnish with quartered apple slices.

Cassoulet

—— SERVES 4–6 ——

100 g/4 oz bacon, rind removed and chopped
450 g/1 lb belly of pork, cubed
4 small chicken quarters
225 g/8 oz cervelat sausage, cubed
225 g/8 oz haricot beans, soaked overnight in
cold water
900 ml/1½ pints chicken stock
225 g/8 oz tomatoes, peeled and chopped
1 bouquet garni
salt and freshly ground black pepper
100 g/4 oz fresh white breadcrumbs

Place the bacon in an ovenproof casserole. Add the belly of pork, chicken quarters and cervelat sausage.

Drain the beans and add to the casserole with the stock and the tomatoes. Add the bouquet garni and season generously. Mix well, cover and cook in a moderate oven (160°C, 325°F, Gas Mark 3) for 1½ hours.

Remove and discard the bouquet garni. If the mixture looks dry add a little more stock. Sprinkle with the breadcrumbs and continue to bake, uncovered, for a further 1 hour.

Savoury meatloaf

SERVES 6–8

2 medium onions, finely chopped
225 g/8 oz button mushrooms, finely chopped
450 g/1 lb minced beef
450 g/1 lb minced pork
225 g/8 oz streaky bacon, rind removed and
minced
1 large clove garlic, crushed
100 g/4 oz fresh white breadcrumbs
3 tablespoons dry white wine or stock
1 (142-ml/5-fl oz) carton soured cream
pinch of ground nutmeg
1 teaspoon curry powder
$\frac{1}{2}$ teaspoon ground allspice
salt and freshly ground black pepper

Place all the ingredients in a bowl, season generously and mix well to blend. Pack into a 1-kg/2-lb loaf tin and cover with foil. Stand in a roasting tin half-full with warm water and bake in a moderately hot oven (190°C, 375°F, Gas Mark 5) for 1 hour.

Remove the foil from the loaf, increase the oven temperature to 200°C, 400°F, Gas Mark 6 and cook for a further 30 minutes.

Remove from the oven, return the foil to the top of the loaf, cool and weigh down overnight in the refrigerator.

To serve, turn the loaf out of the tin, slice and place on a serving dish. Garnish with salad ingredients and serve with spicy chutney and French bread.

Russian salmon pie

SERVES 4

75 g/3 oz butter
1 small onion, finely chopped
100 g/4 oz button mushrooms, sliced
50 g/2 oz flour
300 ml/$\frac{1}{2}$ pint milk
salt and freshly ground black pepper
350 g/12 oz fresh or canned cooked salmon,
flaked
1 hard-boiled egg, chopped
1 (368-g/13-oz) packet frozen puff pastry,
defrosted
beaten egg to glaze

Heat the butter in a saucepan and fry the onion for 5 minutes until soft. Add the mushrooms and fry for 2–3 minutes. Stir in the flour and cook for 1 minute. Gradually add the milk, bring to the boil and cook for 2–3 minutes. Season and stir in the fish and chopped egg and leave to cool.

Roll out the pastry thinly to a 30-cm/12-inch square. Pile the filling in the centre. Brush the edges with beaten egg. Bring the two opposite points of pastry to the centre of the filling and secure. Bring up the other two points and press together to form an envelope shape. Press and secure the seams together. Flute the seams. Decorate the top with pastry leaves made from the pastry trimmings and glaze with the beaten egg.

Place on a dampened baking tray and cook in a hot oven (220°C, 425°F, Gas Mark 7) for 30–40 minutes or until the pastry is crisp and golden brown. Serve hot or cold with a crisp salad.

Spring lamb casserole

SERVES 4–6

4–6 lamb chops
4 onions, sliced
4 small carrots, sliced
600 ml/1 pint stock
salt and freshly ground black pepper
1 teaspoon dried mixed herbs or 1 tablespoon
chopped fresh mixed herbs
225 g/8 oz shelled peas
225 g/8 oz small new potatoes

Trim the chops and arrange in a casserole with the onion, carrots, stock and seasoning to taste. Cover and cook in a moderate oven (160°C, 325°F, Gas Mark 3) for 45 minutes.

Add the herbs, peas and potatoes and cook for a further 50 minutes, or until the meat is cooked and the vegetables are tender. Adjust the seasoning if necessary and serve.

Tagliatelle bolognese

SERVES 4

2 tablespoons oil
1 onion, finely chopped
1 clove garlic, crushed
450 g/1 lb lean minced beef
100 g/4 oz button mushrooms, thinly sliced
2 tablespoons flour
1 (396-g/14-oz) can peeled tomatoes
salt and freshly ground black pepper
1 teaspoon chopped parsley
$\frac{1}{4}$ teaspoon dried mixed herbs
2 teaspoons tomato purée
150 ml/$\frac{1}{4}$ pint red wine
300 ml/$\frac{1}{2}$ pint beef stock
275 g/10 oz tagliatelle or ribbon noodles
15 g/$\frac{1}{2}$ oz butter
75 g/3 oz Parmesan cheese, grated

Heat the oil in a heavy-based saucepan. Add the onion, cover and cook over a low heat until soft but not brown, about 5 minutes. Add the garlic and beef and cook until the meat is well browned, about 10 minutes. Add the mushrooms and cook for a further 2–3 minutes. Stir in the flour and cook for 1 minute. Gradually add the tomatoes and their juice, seasoning to taste, the parsley, mixed herbs and tomato purée. Add the red wine and stock and bring to the boil. Lower the heat and simmer, covered, for 45–50 minutes.

About 15 minutes before the sauce has cooked, plunge the tagliatelle into a large pan of boiling salted water. Bring back to the boil and cook for 12 minutes. Drain and toss in the butter. Season to taste and pile on a warmed serving dish. Pour the sauce over the noodles and serve topped with the Parmesan cheese.

Noisettes of lamb Shrewsbury

—— SERVES 4 ——

65 g/2½ oz butter
1 tablespoon oil
8 noisettes of lamb
mint or watercress sprigs to garnish
SAUCE
40 g/1½ oz butter
1 small carrot, diced
1 small onion, chopped
2 stalks celery, chopped
25 g/1 oz lean bacon, rind removed and chopped
25 g/1 oz flour
600 ml/1 pint stock
300 ml/½ pint red or white wine
2 teaspoons tomato purée
1 bouquet garni
½ teaspoon dried rosemary
3 tablespoons redcurrant jelly
salt and freshly ground black pepper

First prepare the sauce by melting the butter in a heavy-based saucepan. Add the vegetables and bacon and cook for about 10 minutes. Add the flour and cook over a low heat for a further 10 minutes, stirring continuously until the mixture is light brown. Heat the stock and wine together in another saucepan then whisk into the vegetable mixture. Stir in the tomato purée and add the bouquet garni and rosemary. Simmer the sauce over a gentle heat, covered, for 2 hours. Strain through a coarse sieve and skim any fat from the surface. Stir in the redcurrant jelly until melted and season to taste.

Heat the butter and oil in a heavy-based frying pan. Add the noisettes and cook over a moderate heat for 4–6 minutes on each side. Garnish with mint or watercress sprigs and serve with the sauce.

Creamy curried pasta

—— SERVES 4 ——

225 g/8 oz pasta shapes
1 onion, finely chopped
4 tablespoons dry vermouth or stock
150 ml/¼ pint mayonnaise
2 teaspoons mild concentrated curry paste
2 teaspoons apricot jam
2 teaspoons lemon juice
8 large sausages, cooked and thinly sliced
GARNISH
halved tomato slices
chopped parsley

Cook the pasta in boiling salted water for 12–15 minutes, until tender. Drain well and allow to cool.

Place the onion and vermouth or stock in a saucepan and bring to the boil. Simmer for 3 minutes then remove from the heat and allow to cool.

Combine the onion mixture with the mayonnaise, curry paste, apricot jam and lemon juice. Pour over the pasta and toss well to coat. Finally fold in the cooked sausages. Turn the mixture into a serving dish and garnish with the tomatoes and parsley. Chill for 30 minutes before serving.

Chicken rice ring

——— SERVES 4 ———

225 g/8 oz long-grain rice
25 g/1 oz butter or margarine
1 green pepper, deseeded and chopped
1 red pepper, deseeded and chopped
1 onion, chopped
75 g/3 oz frozen sweetcorn kernels, defrosted
salt and freshly ground black pepper
4 chicken portions, cooked
SAUCE
150 ml/¼ pint mayonnaise
2 teaspoons curry paste
2 small onions, grated
2 teaspoons finely chopped parsley
paprika pepper

Cook the rice in boiling salted water according to the packet instructions and drain.

Meanwhile, heat the butter or margarine in a saucepan and add the peppers and chopped onion. Cook gently for 5 minutes. Add the sweetcorn and continue to cook for 5 minutes. Fold into the cooked rice and season to taste. Pack into a greased 1.25-litre/2-pint ring mould, leave to cool then chill.

Meanwhile, remove the skin and any bones from the chicken and cube the flesh. Combine the mayonnaise, curry paste, grated onion, parsley and seasoning to taste. Fold in the cubed chicken meat and chill.

To serve, unmould the rice ring onto a plate and fill the centre with the chicken mixture. Dust with a little paprika pepper and serve.

Bobotie

——— SERVES 4 ———

1 large slice bread, crusts removed
300 ml/½ pint milk
25 g/1 oz butter
1 onion, finely chopped
1 dessert apple, peeled, cored and chopped
1½ teaspoons curry powder
1 tablespoon mango chutney
25 g/1 oz flaked almonds
15 g/½ oz seedless raisins
1 tablespoon lemon juice
450 g/1 lb minced cooked lamb
salt and freshly ground black pepper
2 eggs, beaten
few lemon, lime, orange or bay leaves
parsley sprigs to garnish

Soak the bread in the milk and grease a medium-sized pie dish.

Heat the butter in a saucepan, add the onion and apple and cook for 5 minutes. Stir in the curry powder and continue to cook for 5 minutes. Add the chutney, almonds, raisins and lemon juice.

Squeeze the milk from the bread and add the bread to the lamb, reserving the milk. Fork the bread into the meat and season generously. Add the curried mixture and combine well. Place in the pie dish and cook in a moderate oven (180°C, 350°F, Gas Mark 4) for 15 minutes.

Meanwhile mix the eggs and reserved milk together. Season to taste and pour over the meat mixture. Top with the leaves and bake for a further 45 minutes or until the top is set and lightly browned. Garnish with parsley sprigs and serve hot with rice and a tomato salad.

Lamb casserole with apricots

1 (1.8-kg/4-lb) leg of lamb
2 tablespoons oil
25 g/1 oz butter
$\frac{1}{2}$ teaspoon ground cinnamon
$\frac{1}{2}$ teaspoon ground nutmeg
3 tablespoons flour
600 ml/1 pint chicken stock
juice of 1 large orange
2 teaspoons chopped fresh mint or mint sauce
100 g/4 oz dried apricots, soaked in cold water
overnight
4 medium onions, quartered
salt and freshly ground black pepper
450 g/1 lb potatoes

Remove the meat from the bone and cut into 3.5-cm/ 1$\frac{1}{2}$-inch pieces. Heat the oil and butter in a frying pan and brown the lamb on all sides until golden. Place in a large, shallow flameproof casserole. Add the cinnamon, nutmeg and flour to the pan juices and cook for 2–3 minutes, stirring well. Gradually add the stock, orange juice, mint or mint sauce and drained apricots. Pour over the meat, add the quartered onions and season well.

Cut the peeled potatoes into 5-mm/$\frac{1}{4}$-inch slices and layer on top. Cover with a lid and cook in a cool oven (150°C, 300°F, Gas Mark 2) for about 1$\frac{1}{2}$ hours. Remove the lid and brown for a further 15 minutes.

Cook's Tip

Ring the changes in the above lamb casserole by sub-stituting half of the dried apricots for other dried fruits. Apricot and dried pears, dried apples, dried peaches and dried bananas are all good combinations.

Rabbit with sage dumplings

100 g/4 oz streaky bacon, rind removed and
chopped
4 rabbit portions
4 stalks celery, trimmed and chopped
2 leeks, sliced
1 bay leaf
225 g/8 oz carrots, sliced
2 tablespoons flour
600 ml/1 pint stock
salt and freshly ground black pepper
SAGE DUMPLINGS
75 g/3 oz self-raising flour
40 g/1$\frac{1}{2}$ oz shredded suet
1 teaspoon chopped fresh sage leaves
cold water to mix

Cook the bacon in a flameproof casserole until the fat runs. Add the rabbit and fry gently until lightly browned, about 10 minutes. Stir in the celery, leek, bay leaf and carrot. Shower in the flour and mix well. Cook for 1 minute then gradually add the stock, a little at a time, and bring to the boil, stirring continuously. Season to taste. Cover the casserole and cook in a moderate oven (160°C, 325°F, Gas Mark 3) for 1$\frac{1}{2}$ hours or until the rabbit is tender.

To prepare the dumplings, combine the self-raising flour, suet and sage and season lightly. Mix to a soft dough with cold water. Divide the dumpling dough into four portions then shape evenly into balls and place on top of the casserole. Cover again and cook for a further 20–25 minutes or until the dumplings are well risen and cooked through.

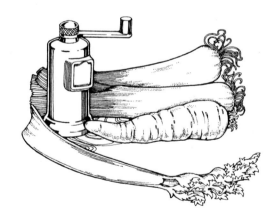

Autumn rabbit casserole

—————— SERVES 4 ——————

2 tablespoons oil
100 g/4 oz streaky bacon, rind removed and diced
1 medium onion, sliced
175 g/6 oz cooking apple, peeled, cored and sliced
675 g/1½ lb firm white cabbage, shredded
salt and freshly ground black pepper
4 rabbit portions
2 tablespoons flour
1½ teaspoons French mustard
150 ml/¼ pint dry cider
250 ml/8 fl oz light stock
chopped parsley to garnish

Heat the oil in a large frying pan and lightly brown the bacon, onion and apple. Remove from the pan with a slotted spoon and mix with the cabbage and a generous amount of seasoning. Pack into the base of a large ovenproof casserole.

Brown the rabbit portions in the remaining pan juices and place on top of the cabbage. Stir the flour and mustard into the pan and cook for 1 minute. Gradually add the cider and stock. Season to taste, bring to the boil and pour over the rabbit. Cover and cook in a moderate oven (160°C, 325°F, Gas Mark 3) for 1¾ hours, or until the rabbit is tender. Check the seasoning and garnish with plenty of chopped parsley.

Liver and bacon provençal

—————— SERVES 4 ——————

450 g/1 lb lamb's liver, sliced into long thick strips
50 g/2 oz seasoned flour
2 tablespoons oil
225 g/8 oz streaky bacon, rind removed and chopped
450 g/1 lb onions, chopped
1 (396-g/14-oz) can peeled tomatoes
1 teaspoon dried marjoram
1 bay leaf
1 tablespoon Worcestershire sauce
450 ml/¾ pint stock
salt and freshly ground black pepper

Coat the liver in the seasoned flour. Heat the oil in a frying pan and fry the liver quickly on all sides until browned. Remove with a slotted spoon and place in a 1.75-litre/3-pint casserole.

Add the bacon and onion to the pan and cook until golden, about 10 minutes. Stir in any remaining seasoned flour and cook for 1 minute. Add the canned tomatoes with their juice, the marjoram, bay leaf and Worcestershire sauce. Add the stock and bring to the boil. Pour over the liver in the casserole. Cover and cook in a cool oven (150°C, 300°F, Gas Mark 2) for about 1½ hours, or until tender. Season to taste and serve with cooked noodles and a green salad.

Salami-stuffed chicken

SERVES 6–8

1 (1.4-kg/3-lb) oven-ready chicken, boned
1 (170-g/6-oz) packet Brussels liver pâté
50 g/2 oz fresh brown breadcrumbs
25 g/1 oz chopped mixed nuts
2 tablespoons chopped parsley
2 tablespoons chopped chives
pinch of ground nutmeg
salt and freshly ground black pepper
1–2 tablespoons milk
100 g/4 oz salami, sliced
2 knackwurst
25 g/1 oz butter
parsley sprigs to garnish

Place the chicken, skin-side down, on a large board. Mix the pâté, breadcrumbs, nuts, parsley, chives, nutmeg and seasoning together well, softening with the milk if necessary. Spread one-third of this pâté mixture over the chicken and arrange the salami on top. Spread over another third of the pâté and cover with the knackwurst, end to end. Top with the final third of pâté.

Sew up the chicken with fine thread to a good shape, enclosing the stuffing, and weigh the bird. Season and dot with the butter. Place in a roasting tin and cook in a moderately hot oven (190°C, 375°F, Gas Mark 5), allowing 25 minutes per 450 g/1 lb, basting from time to time.

When cooked allow to cool, remove the thread and refrigerate. Serve sliced with new potatoes and a mixed salad.

Fruity beef curry

SERVES 4–6

3 tablespoons oil
1 large onion, chopped
900 g/2 lb stewing steak, cubed
4 teaspoons curry powder, hot, medium or mild
according to taste
600 ml/1 pint beef stock
2 tablespoons lemon juice
2 tablespoons peach chutney
50 g/2 oz dried apricots
salt
2 dessert apples, peeled, cored and thinly sliced
2 bananas, thickly sliced
4 tomatoes, peeled and quartered

Heat the oil in a heavy-based saucepan. Add the onion and cook until golden, about 5–8 minutes. Add the beef and cook until browned on all sides. Stir in the curry powder and cook for 2 minutes, stirring constantly. Gradually add the beef stock, lemon juice and chutney and bring to the boil. Stir in the apricots and salt to taste. Reduce the heat, cover and simmer for $1\frac{3}{4}$–2 hours or until the meat is tender.

Add the apples, bananas and tomatoes and continue to simmer for a further 15 minutes. Serve hot with rice and poppadoms.

Pastries and Pies

Cooking food 'en croûte', the French way of saying 'wrapped-up in pastry', keeps in all the succulent juices and flavourings a food can offer. Moreover, prepared this way, simple pieces of meat, fish or poultry and seasoned pâtés or fillings can be made to look splendidly impressive with their decorated handsome crust.

A pie will suit almost any occasion from the simple to the sumptuous and has the added bonus that it can generally be prepared well ahead. Experiment with flours and pastries to give variety–don't just rely upon the traditional shortcrust. Light-as-air puff pastry, nutty wholemeal or substantial hot water crust will all prove welcome changes. Notched and trimmed or decorated with cut-out shapes will also put your original stamp of approval on the dish.

For best results, shortcrust, puff and flaky pastry should be made in a cool rather than hot or steamy kitchen. If you have the time, put all the equipment in the refrigerator for half an hour before you begin. Roll out on a lightly floured work surface. Start with the pastry in roughly the shape required and roll in short sharp strokes in one direction only–away from you. If covering pies, make sure that you position strips of pastry around the pie dish rim for the pastry lid to adhere to. A pie funnel may be used to help hold up the upper crust, but the pastry should not be pierced and the funnel revealed until the pastry has cooked a little to form a high dome.

Pigeon and cranberry pie; Cream cheese and bacon quiche (see overleaf)

Pigeon and cranberry pie

4 pigeons, skinned, boned and chopped
25 g/1 oz seasoned flour
50 g/2 oz butter or margarine
2 onions, chopped
15 g/½ oz flour
300 ml/½ pint chicken stock
225 g/8 oz fresh or defrosted frozen cranberries
25 g/1 oz sugar
grated rind and juice of 1 orange
pinch of dried thyme
salt and freshly ground black pepper
150 ml/¼ pint double cream
1 (368-g/13-oz) packet frozen puff pastry, defrosted
beaten egg to glaze

Toss the pigeon pieces in the seasoned flour. Melt the butter or margarine in a pan and cook the pigeons until browned, about 10–15 minutes. Remove with a slotted spoon and place in a medium-sized casserole dish. Add the onion to the pan juices and cook for 5 minutes. Stir in the flour and cook for 1 minute. Gradually add the stock, cranberries, sugar, orange rind, orange juice and thyme. Season well and pour over the pigeons. Cook, covered, in a moderate oven (180°C, 350°F, Gas Mark 4) for 1 hour. Add the double cream and turn into a 1.25-litre/2-pint pie dish. Leave to cool.

Roll out the pastry on a lightly floured surface until large enough to cover the top of the pie dish. Cut a strip of pastry to fit the rim of the pie dish. Dampen this strip with water and lift the pie lid onto the pie. Trim and flute the edges. Make a small hole in the centre of the pie to allow any steam to escape. Decorate with any pastry trimmings and glaze with beaten egg.

Increase the oven temperature to hot (220°C, 425°F, Gas Mark 7) and bake the pie for 35–40 minutes or until well risen and golden brown.

Cream cheese and bacon quiche

PASTRY
175 g/6 oz plain flour
pinch of salt
85 g/3 oz margarine
2 tablespoons cold water
FILLING
4 rashers smoked streaky bacon, rind removed
1 egg
3 egg yolks
225 g/8 oz cream cheese, softened
150 ml/¼ pint double cream, lightly whipped
salt and freshly ground black pepper
3 tomatoes, peeled and sliced
cooked bacon rolls and parsley sprigs to garnish

First make the pastry by sifting the flour and salt into a mixing bowl. Rub in the margarine until the mixture resembles fine breadcrumbs. Add the water and stir into a dough. Knead on a lightly floured surface until smooth. Roll out the pastry dough and use to line a 20-cm/8-inch flan ring placed on a baking tray. Bake 'blind' in a moderately hot oven (200°C, 400°F, Gas Mark 6) for 10 minutes.

Meanwhile, cut the bacon into thin strips and fry without any fat in a frying pan for about 3 minutes. Drain on absorbent kitchen paper then place in the bottom of the partially cooked flan case.

Beat the egg and egg yolks together then stir into the cream cheese, keeping the mixture smooth. Gradually stir in the cream and season generously. Pour the mixture over the bacon in the flan case and arrange the tomatoes on top.

Continue to bake for a further 20 minutes then reduce the heat to moderate (180°C, 350°F, Gas Mark 4) for a further 10 minutes, or until the mixture is set. Serve the quiche garnished with the bacon rolls and chopped parsley.

Cook's Tip

It is often essential to bake a pastry case 'blind' or without a filling. Baking 'blind' ensures that the pastry base is cooked adequately before the filling is added and the temperature is reduced.

To bake 'blind', line the pastry case with greaseproof paper or foil. Half fill it with uncooked, dried beans. Bake in a moderately hot oven (200°C, 400°F, Gas Mark 6) for 10–15 minutes. If you require a completely cooked empty pastry case to fill later with a ready-cooked filling then remove the beans, paper or foil and bake for a further 5–10 minutes.

Hidden lamb savouries

SERVES 4

25 g/1 oz butter
1 medium onion, chopped
2 lamb's kidneys, cored and chopped
100 g/4 oz mushrooms, thinly sliced
1 tablespoon chopped parsley
½ teaspoon dried tarragon
salt and freshly ground black pepper
3 tablespoons wine or stock
2 tablespoons oil
4 (175-g/6-oz) lamb chump chops
1 (368-g/13-oz) packet frozen puff pastry,
defrosted
beaten egg to glaze

Melt the butter in a saucepan and cook the onion for 5 minutes. Add the kidney and cook for 2–3 minutes. Stir in the mushrooms, parsley, tarragon, seasoning and wine or stock. Cook for 2–3 minutes and leave to cool.

Meanwhile heat the oil in a frying pan and cook the chops for 3 minutes on each side. Allow to cool slightly.

Divide the pastry into four portions and roll out each to make a square large enough to enclose the chops. Spoon a little of the kidney mixture on each square, top with a chop and the remaining kidney mixture. Dampen the edges with water and fold over to enclose the chops. Seal well and trim. Reserve any trimmings to decorate. Glaze with beaten egg.

Place on a dampened baking tray and bake in a hot oven (220°C, 425°F, Gas Mark 7) for 25 minutes. Garnish with parsley and serve with seasonal vegetables.

Cornish pasties

SERVES 4

PASTRY
225 g/8 oz self-raising flour
pinch of salt
110 g/4 oz butter or margarine
2–3 tablespoons cold water
beaten egg to glaze
FILLING
225 g/8 oz lean beef steak
2 medium potatoes, diced
1 medium onion, finely chopped
½ teaspoon dried mixed herbs
1 tablespoon chopped parsley
salt and freshly ground black pepper
1–2 tablespoons stock

Prepare the pastry by sifting the flour into a bowl with the salt. Rub in the butter or margarine. Add enough cold water to make a firm dough.

Shred the meat finely. Mix the meat, potato and onion together with the mixed herbs, parsley, seasoning and enough stock to moisten thoroughly.

Divide the pastry into four portions and roll each out on a lightly floured surface to a circle about 12.5–15 cm/5–6 inches in diameter. Dampen the edges with water. Place one-quarter of the filling on each and draw the pastry over the filling. Crimp the edges and use any pastry trimmings to decorate. Place on a greased baking tray and glaze with the egg. Bake in a moderately hot oven (200°C, 400°F, Gas Mark 6) for 15 minutes. Reduce to moderate (180°C, 350°F, Gas Mark 4) and bake for a further 25–30 minutes. Serve with a salad.

81

Duck and orange pie

—— SERVES 4 ——

1 (1.5-kg/3½-lb) oven-ready duckling
grated rind and juice of 1 orange
2 onions, chopped
175 g/6 oz fresh white breadcrumbs
1 tablespoon chopped fresh sage
salt and freshly ground black pepper
PASTRY
350 g/12 oz plain flour
pinch of salt
85 g/3 oz butter or margarine
85 g/3 oz lard
4–5 tablespoons cold water
beaten egg to glaze

Cut the breast meat from the duckling and cut into thin strips. Mix with the orange rind and juice. Remove the rest of the meat from the carcass, mince the flesh and the giblet liver and place in a bowl with the onion, breadcrumbs, sage and seasoning to taste. Mix well.

Prepare the pastry by sifting the flour and salt into a bowl. Rub in the fats, add the water and mix to a firm dough. Use three-quarters of the dough to line the base and sides of a 15-cm/6-inch round loose-bottomed cake tin.

Put half the minced mixture into the base of the tin. Cover with the sliced breast meat. Top with the remaining minced mixture. Roll out the remaining pastry large enough to cover the top of the pie. Dampen the edges with water, put the lid on the pie, trim and flute the edges. Decorate with any pastry trimmings. Glaze with beaten egg and bake in a moderately hot oven (200°C, 400°F, Gas Mark 6) for 30 minutes. Reduce the oven temperature to moderate (180°C, 350°F, Gas Mark 4) and cook for 1 hour. Remove the pie from the tin, but keep it still on the cake tin base, brush with the egg again and bake for a further 30 minutes. Cool and serve with halved orange slices and watercress sprigs.

Deep fried steak en croûte

—— SERVES 4 ——

25 g/1 oz butter
4 (100-g/4-oz) 'minute' steaks
1 (368-g/13-oz) packet frozen puff pastry, defrosted
1 (150-g/5-oz) can pâté
beaten egg to glaze
flour to dust
oil for deep frying

Melt the butter in a frying pan and fry the steaks for 2 minutes, turning over halfway through the cooking time. Allow to cool slightly.

Roll out the pastry on a lightly floured surface and cut out eight circles of pastry about 2.5 cm/1 inch larger in diameter than the steaks.

Spread a quarter of the pâté onto one side of each steak. Place each steak on a circle of pastry, pâté side down. Brush the edges of the pastry with a little beaten egg and dust with a little flour. Place the second circle of pastry on top and pinch the edges together tightly. Decorate the tops of the croûtes with any pastry trimmings and glaze with the beaten egg.

Heat the oil to 180°C/350°F, or until a cube of day-old bread turns golden in 1 minute. Deep fry the steaks in the hot oil for 4 minutes. Drain on absorbent kitchen paper and serve at once with a mixed salad.

Wholemeal sausage pie

SERVES 6

PASTRY
225 g/8 oz wholemeal flour
pinch of salt
55 g/2 oz butter or margarine
55 g/2 oz lard
3 tablespoons cold water
beaten egg or milk to glaze

FILLING
350 g/12 oz pork sausagemeat
1 small onion, finely chopped
3 tablespoons fresh white breadcrumbs
1 teaspoon dried mixed herbs
2 tomatoes, peeled and chopped
2 hard-boiled eggs, shelled

To make the pastry mix the flour with the salt in a bowl. Rub the butter or margarine and lard into the flour until the mixture resembles fine breadcrumbs. Add the water and mix to a firm but workable dough. Roll out two-thirds of the pastry on a lightly floured surface and use to line a 0.5-kg/1-lb loaf tin.

Prepare the filling by mixing the sausagemeat, onion, breadcrumbs, herbs and tomatoes together. Place half this mixture in the base of the tin. Arrange the two hard-boiled eggs along the centre and cover with the remaining sausagemeat mixture.

Roll out the remaining pastry to form a lid. Dampen the edge of the pastry with water and cover the pie with the pastry lid. Trim and flute the edges. Use any pastry trimmings to make leaves to decorate the top of the pie. Make a small hole in the centre to allow any steam to escape. Brush with beaten egg or milk.

Cook in a moderately hot oven (190°C, 375°F, Gas Mark 5) for 1 hour or until cooked. Serve cold with salad.

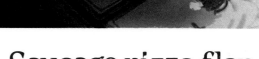

Sausage pizza flan

SERVES 4–6

FILLING
1 onion, finely chopped
25 g/1 oz butter
50 g/2 oz flour
1 (227-g/8-oz) can peeled tomatoes
1 tablespoon tomato ketchup
150 ml/¼ pint milk
¼ teaspoon dried mixed herbs
salt and freshly ground black pepper

SCONE DOUGH
225 g/8 oz self-raising flour
½ teaspoon salt
50 g/2 oz butter
7 tablespoons milk

TOPPING
4 large sausages, cooked and sliced into rings
1 tablespoon chopped parsley
parsley sprigs to garnish

Cook the onion in the butter in a medium-sized saucepan until soft but not brown. Stir in the flour, cook for 1 minute then remove from the heat. Gradually add the canned tomatoes with their juice, the tomato ketchup, milk, herbs and seasoning to taste. Return to the heat, bring to the boil and cook for 2 minutes. Allow to cool.

Make the scone dough by sifting the flour with the salt. Rub in the butter. Add the milk and mix to a soft but workable dough. Turn onto a lightly floured surface and roll out to a rectangle measuring 33 × 23 cm/13 × 9 inches to line a 28 × 18-cm/11 × 7-inch deep Swiss roll tin. Ease into the tin and trim the edges. Pour the filling into the scone case and bake in a moderately hot oven (190°C, 375°F, Gas Mark 5) for 25 minutes. Arrange the sausages down the centre of the flan and sprinkle with chopped parsley. Slice and garnish with parsley sprigs to serve.

Sausage meatloaf in pastry

— SERVES 8 —

25 g/1 oz butter
1 large onion, chopped
450 g/1 lb streaky bacon, rind removed
175 g/6 oz fresh white breadcrumbs
50 g/2 oz shredded beef suet
1 tablespoon chopped parsley
salt and freshly ground black pepper
1 egg, beaten
350 g/12 oz pork sausagemeat
175 g/6 oz cooked chicken meat, sliced
1 (368-g/13-oz) packet frozen puff pastry,
defrosted
beaten egg to glaze

Melt the butter in a saucepan and fry the onion until soft, about 5 minutes. Reserve eight of the bacon rashers and chop the rest quite finely. Add to the onion mixture and cook for a further 5 minutes. Place the breadcrumbs in a bowl, add the suet, parsley, bacon and onion mixture and seasoning to taste. Bind together with the egg.

Stretch the bacon rashers with the back of a knife and use six to line the base and sides of a 1-kg/2-lb loaf tin. Spread half the sausagemeat on the base of the tin and cover with half the chicken. Top with the bacon mixture, the remaining chicken and remaining sausagemeat. Top with the remaining two bacon rashers. Cover with aluminium cooking foil and stand in a roasting tin half-full with warm water. Bake in a moderate oven (180°C, 350°F, Gas Mark 4) for 1½ hours. Remove and leave until cold.

Roll out the pastry on a lightly floured surface to a rectangle large enough to enclose the meatloaf. Brush with a little of the beaten egg. Place the meatloaf on the pastry, egg side in, and completely enclose the meatloaf in the pastry. Seal the edges well, reserving any pastry trimmings. Glaze the pastry again with the beaten egg and decorate with the pastry trimmings.

Place on a dampened baking tray and bake in a hot oven (220°C, 425°F, Gas Mark 7) for 35–40 minutes until golden brown and well risen. Serve sliced cold with salads.

Bacon and sage plait

— SERVES 4–6 —

40 g/1½ oz butter or margarine
2 onions, chopped
225 g/8 oz gammon or collar bacon, rind
removed and cut into 5-mm/¼-inch pieces
100 g/4 oz mushrooms, thinly sliced
225 g/8 oz pork sausagemeat
1 egg, beaten
½ teaspoon dried thyme
1 tablespoon chopped parsley
2 teaspoons chopped chives
1 teaspoon chopped fresh sage
salt and freshly ground black pepper
1 (368-g/13-oz) packet frozen puff pastry,
defrosted
beaten egg to glaze
watercress sprigs to garnish

Melt the butter or margarine in a saucepan. Add the onion and cook for 5 minutes. Add the bacon and fry gently for 10 minutes. Stir in the mushrooms and continue cooking for a further 5 minutes. Combine in a bowl with the sausagemeat, egg, herbs and seasoning.

Roll out the pastry on a lightly floured surface to an oblong approximately 30 × 20 cm/12 × 8 inches. Fold in half lengthways and make diagonal cuts 5 cm/2 inches in from the joined long edge of the pastry. Place on a dampened baking tray and open out the pastry. Spoon the prepared filling in a roll shape down the length of the pastry. Fold over the pastry strips in a lattice design and secure together with a little beaten egg. Glaze with the beaten egg and bake in a hot oven (220°C, 425°F, Gas Mark 7) for 30–40 minutes until cooked, crisp and golden. Serve garnished with watercress sprigs.

Chicken and ham turnovers

MAKES 6

40 g/1½ oz butter or margarine
1 medium onion, chopped
50 g/2 oz mushrooms, coarsely chopped
40 g/1½ oz flour
300 ml/½ pint milk
1 teaspoon French mustard
salt and freshly ground black pepper
175 g/6 oz cooked chicken meat, coarsely
chopped
100 g/4 oz cooked ham, cubed
1 (368-g/13-oz) packet frozen puff pastry,
defrosted
beaten egg to glaze

Melt the butter or margarine in a small saucepan. Add the onion and mushrooms and cook gently for 2 minutes until beginning to soften. Stir in the flour and cook for 1 minute. Gradually add the milk to make a sauce. Bring to the boil, stirring, then reduce the heat and cook for 2 minutes. Remove from the heat, add the mustard, seasoning to taste, chicken and ham. Leave to cool.

Roll out the pastry on a lightly floured surface to a 30 × 45-cm/12 × 18-inch rectangle and cut into six 15-cm/6-inch squares. Divide the chicken mixture into six portions. Pile onto the pastry squares, brush the edges with beaten egg and press together over the filling, sealing the edges well to form a triangle. Cut two slits in the top of the turnovers to allow any steam to escape. Use any pastry trimmings to decorate the turnovers. Glaze with beaten egg, place on a dampened baking tray and bake in a hot oven (220°C, 425°F, Gas Mark 7) for 25–35 minutes until golden brown and cooked through. Serve with a crisp salad.

Festival pie

SERVES 6

1 (1.4-kg/3-lb) lean bacon collar joint
450 g/1 lb carrots, diced
salt and freshly ground black pepper
50 g/2 oz butter
450 g/1 lb onions, thinly sliced into rings
50 g/2 oz flour
1 (326-g/11½-oz) can sweetcorn kernels
about 750 ml/1¼ pints milk
oil to brush
TOPPING
350 g/12 oz self-raising flour
½ teaspoon salt
85 g/3 oz margarine
milk to mix

Place the bacon in a saucepan. Cover with cold water and slowly bring to the boil. Simmer for about 1½ hours, drain and cool. When cool cut into bite-sized cubes.

Meanwhile cook the carrots in boiling salted water until tender, about 10–12 minutes. Drain.

Melt the butter, reserve 16 slices of onion and add the rest to the butter. Cook until soft. Stir in the flour and cook for 2 minutes. Drain the sweetcorn and make the can liquid up to 900 ml/1½ pints with milk. Add this to the flour mixture to make a sauce. Bring to the boil, stirring, then simmer until thickened. Fold in the cooked carrot, sweetcorn and bacon. Season to taste and place in a 3-litre/5-pint ovenproof dish.

Make the topping by sifting the flour with the salt. Rub in the margarine. Add enough milk to bind the ingredients into a light scone dough. Roll out to 1 cm/½ inch thick. Cut out 16 (5-cm/2-inch) rounds with a pastry cutter. Lay an onion slice on the top of each and arrange, overlapping over the bacon mixture. Brush lightly with oil. Bake in a hot oven (230°C, 450°F, Gas Mark 8) for about 30 minutes.

Pork and sage parcels

——— SERVES 4 ———

4 pork chump chops, cut 1 cm/$\frac{1}{2}$ inch thick
1 (368-g/13-oz) packet frozen puff pastry,
defrosted
salt and freshly ground black pepper
1 teaspoon dried sage
25 g/1 oz liver pâté
4 slices mature Cheddar cheese
beaten egg to glaze

Trim any excess fat from the chops. Divide the pastry into four portions and roll each portion out, on a lightly floured surface, until it is large enough to wrap around a chop. Place one chop in the centre of each rolled out piece of pastry, season generously and top with the sage. Cover with the pâté and a slice of cheese. Wrap the pastry around the chop and its filling to completely enclose, sealing the edges with the beaten egg. Reserve any pastry trimmings to decorate the parcels.

Place on a dampened baking tray. Glaze with the beaten egg and decorate with the pastry trimmings. Bake in a hot oven (220°C, 425°F, Gas Mark 7) for 35–40 minutes, until golden. Serve with salad ingredients or seasonal vegetables and garnish with sprigs of parsley.

Steak and kidney pie

——— SERVES 4 ———

675 g/1$\frac{1}{2}$ lb stewing steak, cubed
225 g/8 oz ox kidney, cored and chopped
25 g/1 oz seasoned flour
1 medium onion, sliced
100 g/4 oz button mushrooms
300 ml/$\frac{1}{2}$ pint beef stock
salt and freshly ground black pepper
1 (368-g/13-oz) packet frozen puff pastry,
defrosted
beaten egg to glaze

Toss the steak and kidney in the seasoned flour. Place in a large saucepan with the onion, mushrooms and stock. Season to taste, cover and simmer for 1$\frac{1}{2}$–2 hours, until the meat is tender. Add more stock if necessary. Cool and place in a 900-ml/1$\frac{1}{2}$-pint pie dish.

Roll out the pastry on a lightly floured surface until large enough to cover the top of the pie dish. Cut a strip of pastry to line the rim of the dish. Dampen the strip with water and place the top on the pie. Seal and flute the edges. Make a hole in the centre of the pie to allow any steam to escape. Decorate with any pastry trimmings and glaze with beaten egg.

Bake in a hot oven (220°C, 425°F, Gas Mark 7) for 35–40 minutes, or until golden and well risen.

Vegetarian Dishes

Combine the simplest of ingredients like vegetables, eggs, cereals or pasta — spice them up with a sprinkling of herbs, a little grated cheese or some exotic spices and you have the makings of many a nourishing main dish without meat.

While obviously having special interest to vegetarians they are also eminently suitable for general family eating—especially when animal protein costs continue to soar in price. Tempt the family with an authentic *Vegetarian curry*, a healthy *Wholemeal pizza* or *Hearty Spanish omelette*—they really won't miss the meat.

For those who are following a vegetarian diet the recipes have been devised to contain a substantial proportion of the necessary proteins for good health as well as the essential vitamins and minerals. For those who aren't, this section should prove an inspiration to jaded palates at little cost and ring the changes in what can become a monotonous meat and two vegetable diet.

Baked stuffed onions; Vegetarian curry (see overleaf)

Baked stuffed onions

4 large onions
50 g/2 oz shelled hazelnuts
50 g/2 oz salted peanuts
150 g/5 oz long-grain rice, cooked
225 g/8 oz tomatoes, peeled and coarsely
chopped
$\frac{1}{2}$ teaspoon dried basil
$\frac{1}{4}$ teaspoon dried oregano
1 teaspoon turmeric powder
salt and freshly ground black pepper
50 g/2 oz butter, melted

Boil the onions in their skins for 45–50 minutes until very tender. Cool.

Brown the hazelnuts and peanuts in a hot oven (220°C, 425°F, Gas Mark 7) for 10–15 minutes. Remove and chop finely.

Mix the rice, tomatoes, nuts, herbs, turmeric and seasoning to taste. Slice off the tip and root of each onion but leave on the coloured outer skin. Down one side of each onion cut through to the centre from the top to the bottom. Gently ease the onions open.

Divide the stuffing mixture between the four onions and place in a roasting tin. Pour over the melted butter, cover and bake in a moderately hot oven (200°C, 400°F, Gas Mark 6) for about 40 minutes.

Variations

The above rice, nut and herb stuffing can also be used to fill tomatoes, courgettes or aubergines:
Baked stuffed tomatoes: Cut the caps off the tomatoes from the stem end and reserve. Carefully scoop out the seeds and pulp using a teaspoon and discard. Stuff with the prepared mixture and bake as above. Sufficient for four medium tomatoes.
Baked stuffed courgettes: Cut the courgettes in half lengthways. Scoop out the inner flesh and chop finely. Add to the stuffing and use to fill the courgette cases. Bake as above. Sufficient for six medium courgettes.
Baked stuffed aubergines: Cut the aubergines in half lengthways. Scoop out the inner flesh and chop finely, add to the stuffing. Bake the aubergine cases in a hot oven (220°C, 425°F, Gas Mark 7) for 10 minutes. Fill with the stuffing and bake as above.

Vegetarian curry

4 tablespoons oil
1 teaspoon mustard seeds, crushed
1 (5-cm/2-inch) piece fresh root ginger, minced
2 cloves garlic, crushed
1 onion, minced
1 green chilli, minced
$1\frac{1}{2}$ teaspoons turmeric powder
1 tablespoon ground coriander
675 g/1$\frac{1}{2}$ lb mixed vegetables (carrots, celery, beans, aubergines, cauliflower, green pepper, potatoes, button onions and okra for example), chopped
1 teaspoon salt
225 g/8 oz fresh coconut, puréed in a blender
with 175 ml/6 fl oz water
2 tablespoons chopped fresh coriander leaves
(optional)

Heat the oil in a large saucepan. Add the mustard seeds, ginger and garlic and fry for 1 minute. Add the onion and green chilli and fry gently for 10 minutes, or until the onion is golden. Stir in the turmeric and ground coriander and cook for 1 minute. Add the vegetables and stir well to blend with the fried spices. Stir in the salt and coconut purée. If the mixture looks too dry add 2 tablespoons water.

Cover the pan and simmer for 30 minutes. Turn into a warmed serving dish, sprinkle with the chopped coriander leaves, if used, and serve with rice and sweet pickle.

Cook's Tip

Try serving your curry with some typical Indian accompaniments:
Poppadums: Crispy fried circles of unleavened dough that look and taste similar to giant crisps.
Chapatis: Flat pancakes made from brown flour.
Cucumber raita: A combination of natural yogurt and chopped or grated cucumber.
Bananas: Served sliced and marinated in lime or lemon juice.
Coconut rice: Rice boiled with creamed coconut. Allow 50 g/2 oz of creamed coconut per 225 g/8 oz raw long-grain rice.

Wholemeal pizza

SERVES 4–6

DOUGH BASE
15 g/$\frac{1}{2}$ oz fresh yeast
$\frac{1}{2}$ teaspoon sugar
150 ml/$\frac{1}{4}$ pint lukewarm water
200 g/7 oz wholemeal flour
1 teaspoon salt
$\frac{1}{2}$ tablespoon olive oil
TOPPING
1 (396-g/14-oz) can peeled tomatoes, drained
salt and freshly ground black pepper
1 tablespoon dried basil
$\frac{1}{2}$ teaspoon garlic salt
175 g/6 oz Mozzarella cheese, sliced
8 black olives
1 tablespoon capers

Grease a baking tray then prepare the dough base. Crumble the yeast into a small bowl. Mix with the sugar and 2 tablespoons of the water. Leave until frothy.

Combine the flour and salt in a large mixing bowl. Make a well in the centre and pour in the yeast mixture, olive oil and remaining water. Draw the flour into the liquid and mix to a smooth dough. Knead for 5 minutes. Place back in the clean bowl, cover with a damp cloth and leave to rise in a warm place until double in size.

Roll the dough into a circle 23 cm/9 inches in diameter. Lift onto the baking tray and leave for 10 minutes.

Arrange the sliced tomatoes on the dough, season and sprinkle with the basil and garlic salt. Top with the cheese, olives and capers. Bake in a moderately hot oven (190°C, 375°F, Gas Mark 5) for 30 minutes.

Vegetable lasagne

SERVES 4

175 g/6 oz lasagne verde
2 medium onions, sliced
350 g/12 oz tomatoes, peeled and sliced
350 g/12 oz courgettes, halved lengthways
and sliced
1 tablespoon oil
$\frac{1}{2}$ teaspoon dried basil
1 tablespoon tomato purée
salt and freshly ground black pepper
25 g/1 oz walnut pieces, chopped
1 (454-g/16-oz) carton natural yogurt
2 eggs
$\frac{1}{4}$ teaspoon ground cumin
75 g/3 oz Cheddar cheese, grated
2 tablespoons oil

Cook the lasagne in boiling salted water for about 15 minutes. Drain. Fry the onion, tomatoes and half the courgettes in the 1 tablespoon oil until the tomatoes begin to break down. Stir in the basil, tomato purée and seasoning to taste. Mix in the walnuts.

Grease a 2-litre/3$\frac{1}{2}$-pint deep-sided dish and layer the vegetable mixture and lasagne, ending with a layer of lasagne. Season the yogurt generously and beat in the eggs, cumin and cheese. Pour over the lasagne and top with the remaining courgettes. Brush with the oil and bake in a moderately hot oven (200°C, 400°F, Gas Mark 6) for about 40 minutes until set.

91

Cheese charlotte

—— SERVES 4 ——

1 teaspoon oil
1 thick slice bread, cubed
200 ml/7 fl oz milk
8 slices bread, crusts removed
40 g/1½ oz butter or margarine
3 eggs, separated
1½ tablespoons flour
225 g/8 oz Cheddar cheese, grated
½ teaspoon salt
¼ teaspoon ground nutmeg
100 ml/4 fl oz single cream

Lightly grease a 20-cm/8-inch straight-sided deep baking dish or casserole dish with the oil and set aside.

Place the bread cubes in a shallow dish and sprinkle over half the milk. Place the bread slices in another shallow dish and sprinkle over the remaining milk. Leave both the bread cubes and slices to soak.

In a large mixing bowl, cream the butter or margarine until soft. Mix in the egg yolks, one at a time. Stir in the flour, the soaked bread cubes, cheese, salt and nutmeg. Blend well and stir in the cream.

Whisk the egg whites until stiff then carefully fold into the cheese mixture with a metal spoon.

Line the prepared dish with the soaked bread slices and pour the cheese mixture into the centre. Bake in a moderately hot oven (200°C, 400°F, Gas Mark 6) for 50 minutes or until the charlotte is well puffed and golden. Serve hot with a tomato salad.

Noodle savoury

—— SERVES 6 ——

150 ml/¼ pint olive oil
4 medium onions, thinly sliced
3 cloves garlic, crushed
2 large green peppers, deseeded and sliced
350 g/12 oz mushrooms, thinly sliced
salt and freshly ground black pepper
2 teaspoons dried oregano
250 ml/8 fl oz light stock
6 tablespoons tomato purée
675 g/1½ lb ribbon noodles
50 g/2 oz Parmesan cheese, grated

Heat the oil in a large saucepan. Add the onion, garlic and green pepper. Fry for 5 minutes or until the onion is soft. Add the mushrooms and cook for 2–3 minutes. Stir in seasoning to taste, the oregano and stock. Bring to the boil and stir in the tomato purée. Simmer for 15 minutes.

Meanwhile, cook the noodles in plenty of boiling salted water for 10–12 minutes, until tender. Drain well and arrange on a flameproof serving dish. Pour over the sauce and sprinkle with the grated Parmesan cheese.

Vegetable rissoles

SERVES 4

100 g/4 oz red lentils, soaked overnight, cooked
and drained
1 large onion, finely chopped
1 stalk celery, finely diced
2 small carrots, grated
50 g/2 oz French beans, cooked and finely
chopped
50 g/2 oz fresh white breadcrumbs
3 eggs, beaten
$1\frac{1}{2}$ teaspoons salt
1 teaspoon freshly ground black pepper
1 teaspoon dried mixed herbs
75 g/3 oz dry white breadcrumbs
4 tablespoons oil
watercress sprigs or celery leaves to garnish

Place the lentils, onion, celery, carrot, beans, fresh
breadcrumbs, two of the eggs, the salt, pepper and mixed
herbs in a large bowl. Mix well and leave for 30 minutes.

Shape the mixture into eight small cakes. Dip each
rissole into the remaining beaten egg and then into the
dry breadcrumbs.

Heat the oil in a frying pan and fry the rissoles on
each side for about 7 minutes or until golden. Drain on
absorbent kitchen paper before serving with a home-
made tomato sauce. Garnish with sprigs of watercress or
celery leaves.

Spiced egg ragoût

SERVES 4

50 g/2 oz butter or margarine
225 g/8 oz button onions, halved
450 g/1 lb potatoes, cut into finger-sized pieces
1 teaspoon chilli seasoning
1 teaspoon ground cardamom
$\frac{1}{2}$ teaspoon ground coriander
$\frac{1}{2}$ teaspoon turmeric powder
2 tablespoons flour
1 (396-g/14-oz) can peeled tomatoes
1 clove garlic, crushed
300 ml/$\frac{1}{2}$ pint stock
1 (150-g/5.3-oz) carton natural yogurt
salt and freshly ground black pepper
8 hard-boiled eggs, shelled
GARNISH
fried bread croûtons
1 tablespoon chopped parsley

Heat the butter in a large saucepan. Add the onions and
potatoes and lightly brown. Add the chilli seasoning,
cardamom, coriander, turmeric and flour and cook for 1
minute, stirring all the time.

Add the tomatoes with their can juice, the garlic,
stock, yogurt and seasoning to taste. Bring to the boil,
then cover and simmer gently for about 40 minutes.

Cut the eggs in half lengthways. Add to the sauce and
leave over a low heat to warm through. Mix the croûtons
with the chopped parsley and use to garnish the dish.
Serve with cooked rice or pasta.

Hearty Spanish omelette

4 eggs, beaten
1 tablespoon water
salt and freshly ground black pepper
1 teaspoon lemon juice
25 g/1 oz butter
1 teaspoon oil
1 onion, sliced
1 green pepper, deseeded and sliced
1 cooked potato, diced
2 tomatoes, peeled and sliced

Mix the eggs, water, seasoning to taste and lemon juice together in a bowl. Set aside.

Melt the butter and oil in a 20-cm/8-inch frying pan. Add the onion, green pepper and potato. Fry gently until soft, about 10 minutes. Add the tomatoes, cook for 2–3 minutes then pour on the beaten egg mixture.

Using a fork, stir the mixture gently in the pan to help the egg set evenly. When the mixture is beginning to set, stop stirring and allow the underneath of the omelette to brown. Place under a preheated grill until brown and cooked on top. Cut in half and serve immediately.

Cook's Tip

To ensure that your omelettes never stick, it is essential to 'season' a new omelette or crêpe pan:

Fill the pan with oil and heat it gently. Turn the heat off and allow the oil-filled pan to stand for 24 hours. Remove the oil and wipe the pan clean with absorbent kitchen paper. *Never* wash the inside of the pan—just wipe it clean with kitchen paper. Should the pan become very dirty then rub it with salt, wipe with a damp cloth and then oil again lightly.

Pipérade

3 tablespoons oil
1 medium onion, thinly sliced
2 cloves garlic, crushed
1 medium green pepper, deseeded and sliced
1 medium red pepper, deseeded and sliced
4 large tomatoes, peeled, deseeded and chopped
$\frac{1}{2}$ teaspoon dried thyme
$\frac{1}{2}$ teaspoon dried oregano
salt and freshly ground black pepper
4 large eggs, beaten

In a large, deep frying pan heat the oil. Add the onion, garlic and peppers and cook for 5–7 minutes until soft but not browned. Add the tomatoes, thyme, oregano and seasoning to taste. Cook for 10 minutes.

Pour in the eggs and continue cooking, stirring constantly, for 5–6 minutes, or until the eggs are cooked and set. Transfer to a warmed serving dish and serve.

Variation

Ranch-style eggs
The above recipe can also be used to produce Ranch-style eggs—a light main dish that is said to have originated in the mid-west.

Cook the onion, garlic, peppers, tomatoes with their seasonings as above. Carefully make four hollows in the mixture with a spoon and break each whole egg into the hollow. Cook over a gentle heat for 3–5 minutes until the eggs are just set. Garnish with croûtons made by frying cubes or pieces of bread in equal quantities of hot butter and oil. Serve at once.

Gloucester pie

— SERVES 4 —

75 g/3 oz butter
8 slices bread, crusts removed
100 g/4 oz Double Gloucester cheese, thinly
sliced
225 g/8 oz tomatoes, peeled and sliced
150 ml/¼ pint milk
1 egg, beaten
1 teaspoon prepared mustard
salt and freshly ground black pepper
watercress sprigs to garnish

Butter the slices of bread thickly with three-quarters of the butter. Sandwich together, in pairs, with the cheese and tomato. Cut each sandwich into four triangles and arrange in a shallow ovenproof dish.

Beat the milk, egg, mustard and seasoning to taste together. Pour over the bread and leave to soak for 30 minutes. Dot the top with the remaining butter and bake in a moderately hot oven (190°C, 375°F, Gas Mark 5) for 25–30 minutes or until the top is crisp and golden. Serve garnished with watercress sprigs.

Macaroni redskins

— SERVES 3 —

6 large firm tomatoes
50 g/2 oz quick-cook macaroni
15 g/½ oz butter
1 teaspoon flour
175 ml/6 fl oz milk
2 teaspoons Dijon mustard
50 g/2 oz Cheddar cheese, grated
salt and freshly ground black pepper
fried bread rounds to serve

Cut the caps off the tomatoes from the stem end, using a serrated knife, and reserve. Carefully scoop out the seeds and pulp using a teaspoon and discard. Cook the macaroni in boiling salted water for 5 minutes then drain thoroughly.

Melt the butter in a small saucepan, add the flour and cook for 1 minute. Gradually stir in the milk to make a smooth sauce. Add the mustard, cheese, cooked macaroni and seasoning to taste. Divide the filling among the tomatoes and replace their caps. Place on a baking tray and bake in a moderate oven (180°C, 350°F, Gas Mark 4) for 10 minutes. Serve at once on fried bread rounds.

Chinese spring rolls

SERVES 4

3 tablespoons oil
1 onion, thinly sliced
175 g/6 oz mushrooms, sliced
1 tablespoon soy sauce
1 tablespoon cold water
1 tablespoon cider vinegar
100 g/4 oz canned bean sprouts
2 tablespoons blanched almonds, toasted
SPRING ROLLS
oil for deep frying
100 g/4 oz pancake batter *(see Vegetable pancakes, page 62)*
100 g/4 oz canned bean sprouts
1 small onion, very finely chopped
3 stalks celery, very finely chopped
$\frac{1}{4}$ teaspoon ground ginger
2 egg whites

First prepare the spring rolls. With a pastry brush, lightly coat a small frying pan with a little oil. When hot drop 3–4 tablespoons of the pancake batter into the pan. Cook for 2–3 minutes, turn over and cook the underside. Cook seven more pancakes the same way.

In a mixing bowl, combine the beansprouts, onion, celery and ginger and mix well. Spoon about 1 tablespoon of the stuffing onto the centre of each pancake and roll up, making sure that the filling is completely enclosed. Brush each roll with egg white and set aside.

Heat the oil to 180°C/350°F. Deep fry the rolls for 3 minutes until golden brown. Keep warm.

In a large frying pan prepare the vegetables to accompany the spring rolls. Heat the oil, add the onion and cook for 5 minutes. Add the mushrooms and cook for 3 minutes. Stir in the soy sauce, water and vinegar and cook for 1 minute. Stir in the beansprouts and bring to the boil. Sprinkle with the almonds and serve with the pancake rolls. Garnish with celery leaves.

Pasta omelette

SERVES 2

100 g/4 oz wholemeal pasta shapes
6 eggs
1 tablespoon water
salt and freshly ground black pepper
50 g/2 oz Mozzarella cheese, cubed
2 tomatoes, peeled, deseeded and chopped
4 tablespoons olive oil

Cook the pasta in boiling salted water for 12–15 minutes or until tender. Drain and keep warm.

Beat together the eggs, water and seasoning to taste. Stir in the cheese cubes and tomatoes.

Heat the oil in a large omelette pan. Pour in the egg mixture. Cook over a moderate heat for 4 minutes, lifting the set edges of the omelette to allow the liquid egg mixture to cook. Spoon the pasta onto one half of the omelette and gently fold the other half over. Cook for a further 2 minutes.

Remove from the heat and cook under a preheated hot grill for 2 minutes until the top is golden brown. Serve at once.

Outdoor Main Meals

There is something irresistibly festive about eating out of doors. Perhaps it is the impromptu and alfresco nature of the meal, the sight and aroma of food sizzling over a hot grill or spread like a feast over a hastily-laid cloth.

There is nothing very difficult about preparing main meals out of doors and nothing more delicious. Try cooking skewered food over a barbecue; grills and roasts on a camping or portable stove; tossing a crisp salad on a picnic; or packing away a light-as-air pie for a day at the coast. Extras like chilled wines and drinks, cool simple salads and oven-fresh breads all add up to perfect food for lazy days.

Perhaps it is the open air that sharpens appetites but you will be well advised to think of average indoor helpings and then to double them. But don't despair with the thought of additional work, there are generally plenty of willing hands to help at a barbecue and the most reluctant of cooks will generally lend a hand at out-of-door cooking activities.

There is nothing quite like the marvellous taste of meat, fish or vegetables cooked out of doors, but food from the kitchen can be just as juicy, tender and full of flavour. So should the weather take a turn for the worse don't abandon your food plans for the recipes in this section will taste just as good indoors.

Pork kebabs with spicy orange sauce; Mackerel with cider and rosemary marinade (see overleaf)

Pork kebabs with spicy orange sauce

SERVES 4

675 g/1½ lb pork tenderloin
8 small button onions
6–8 prunes, soaked
4 bay leaves
oil to baste
ORANGE SAUCE
175 g/6 oz soft brown sugar
1 (178-ml/6¼-fl oz) can frozen concentrated
unsweetened orange juice, defrosted
4 tablespoons Worcestershire sauce
juice of 1 lemon
1 teaspoon prepared mustard
1 tablespoon cornflour
2 tablespoons water

Trim the pork and cut into bite-sized cubes. Thread equally onto four skewers with the onions, prunes and bay leaves, alternating the ingredients. Brush with oil and cook under a hot grill, turning occasionally, for 20 minutes.

Meanwhile, put all the sauce ingredients into a pan. Heat gently to dissolve the sugar then bring to the boil, stirring continuously until a smooth sauce is produced. Simmer gently until the kebabs are cooked. Serve the kebabs on rice with the spicy orange sauce.

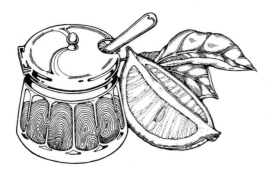

Mackerel with cider and rosemary marinade

SERVES 4

4 medium mackerel, gutted and cleaned
150 ml/¼ pint dry cider
2 tablespoons finely chopped fresh rosemary
salt and freshly ground black pepper
watercress sprigs to garnish

Cut about four deep diagonal slashes into each side of the mackerel. Place in a shallow dish and pour over the cider. Sprinkle with the rosemary and seasoning to taste. Leave to marinate for 2–3 hours, turning from time to time.

Remove from the marinade and cook under a moderate grill or over medium coals on a barbecue, for about 6 minutes each side, basting with the marinade during cooking. Serve on a bed of lettuce leaves, garnish with watercress and accompany with any remaining marinade.

Cook's Tip

It is often difficult to cook fish properly over a barbecue –a too fierce heat can often mean a too crisp skin with an undercooked inner flesh. The perfect way to avoid this is to cook the fish in envelopes of foil or 'en papillote' as the French call it.

To make a papillote, fold a sheet of foil in half, making sure that it is large enough to hold the fish. Cut carefully into a heart shape, which is fatter at one end than the other. Grease the foil and place the fish in the envelope with its seasonings and marinade. Seal the edges by crimping them into small pleats. Finish the parcel by a small twist at the end. Cook as above.

Red mullet, trout, bream, sardines or sea bass are all delicious cooked with the same marinade as the mackerel above.

Cucumber mousse with ham

SERVES 4–6

$\frac{1}{2}$ (127-g/4$\frac{1}{2}$-oz) packet lemon-flavoured jelly
150 ml/$\frac{1}{4}$ pint boiling water
1 cucumber
salt and freshly ground white pepper
2 (225-g/8-oz) cartons cottage cheese
150 ml/$\frac{1}{4}$ pint mayonnaise or soured cream
6 tablespoons cold water
15 g/$\frac{1}{2}$ oz powdered gelatine
lemon juice to taste
8 slices cooked ham

Dissolve the jelly in the boiling water and cool. Spoon a little of the jelly into the base of a 900-ml/1$\frac{1}{2}$-pint ring mould. Thinly slice a quarter of the cucumber and quarter each slice. Arrange in the jelly in the mould and leave until set.

Peel the remaining cucumber, chop coarsely and place in a colander. Sprinkle with salt and leave for 1 hour to drain. Rinse and pat dry on kitchen paper.

Press the cottage cheese through a fine sieve. Stir in the mayonnaise or soured cream. Place the cold water in a small saucepan, sprinkle over the gelatine and stir to dissolve over a low heat. Cool slightly then stir into the cheese mixture with the remaining jelly. Add seasoning and lemon juice to taste then fold in the chopped cucumber. Pour into the mould and leave to set.

To serve, turn the mousse out of the mould. Arrange the rolled slices of ham in the centre of the mousse.

Chicken pâté pie

SERVES 6–8

PASTRY
450 g/1 lb plain flour
pinch of salt
225 g/8 oz margarine
5–6 tablespoons cold water
beaten egg to glaze

FILLING
1 (1.25-kg/2$\frac{1}{2}$-lb) chicken, cooked
75 g/3 oz butter
75 g/3 oz flour
600 ml/1 pint chicken stock
salt and freshly ground black pepper
350 g/12 oz liver sausage
1 (184-g/6$\frac{1}{2}$-oz) can sweet red peppers, sliced

Prepare the pastry by sifting the flour with the salt. Rub in the margarine. Add sufficient cold water to mix to a firm but workable dough.

Prepare the filling by skinning the chicken and carving the flesh into thick slices. Melt the butter, add the flour and cook for 2 minutes. Stir in the stock to make a thick sauce. Season to taste, add the chicken and cool.

Roll out two-thirds of the pastry large enough to line the base and sides of a 21-cm/8$\frac{1}{2}$-inch loose-bottomed spring-release cake tin. Place the liver sausage, in small balls, over the base of the tin. Cover with the peppers and the chicken mixture. Top with the remaining pastry, rolled out to fit. Crimp the edges, make a small hole in the top to allow any steam to escape and decorate with any pastry trimmings. Glaze with egg and bake at 200°C, 400°F, Gas Mark 6 for about 1$\frac{1}{4}$ hours.

Minced beef shasliks

SERVES 4

450 g/1 lb lean finely minced beef
1 teaspoon salt
½ teaspoon freshly ground black pepper
1 tablespoon grated onion
1 tablespoon Worcestershire sauce
4 large onions
8 bay leaves
oil to baste

Combine the beef, salt, pepper, grated onion and Worcestershire sauce in a bowl. Shape into small balls, with wet hands, to the size of a large walnut. Blanch the onions in boiling water for 2–3 minutes, then cut into quarters.

Thread the meatballs, onion quarters and bay leaves onto four skewers, alternating the ingredients. Brush with oil and cook under a moderate grill or on a barbecue over medium coals for 15–20 minutes until cooked. Serve with grilled tomatoes and a crisp salad.

Devilled chicken legs

SERVES 4

1 small glass sherry, about 100 ml/4 fl oz
1 tablespoon tarragon vinegar
2 teaspoons Worcestershire sauce
2 teaspoons prepared English mustard
salt and freshly ground black pepper
4 chicken legs or 8 chicken drumsticks
oil to baste

Mix the sherry, vinegar, Worcestershire sauce, mustard and seasoning to taste together in a small bowl. Make a few neat deep cuts in the chicken flesh and place in a shallow dish. Pour over the sherry mixture and leave the chicken to marinate for at least 1 hour, turning from time to time in the mixture.

Cook the chicken under a moderate grill or on a barbecue over medium coals for 10–15 minutes each side, depending upon size, basting alternately with the sherry mixture and oil. Serve hot accompanied with salad ingredients and pickle.

Honey barbecued chicken

SERVES 4

50 g/2 oz butter
1 medium onion, chopped
1 clove garlic, crushed (optional)
1 (396-g/14-oz) can peeled tomatoes
2 tablespoons Worcestershire sauce
2 tablespoons honey
salt and freshly ground black pepper
4 large or 8 small chicken drumsticks
watercress sprigs to garnish

Place the butter, onion, garlic, tomatoes with their can juice, Worcestershire sauce, honey and seasoning to taste in a small saucepan. Gently heat together for 30 minutes.

Place the drumsticks on a grill pan under a moderate grill, or on a barbecue over medium coals. Brush with the sauce and cook for 10–15 minutes on each side, depending upon size, brushing frequently with the sauce. Serve any remaining sauce separately with the cooked chicken, garnish with watercress and accompany with a rice and vegetable salad.

Malaysian dindings duck

SERVES 4

1 tablespoon ground coriander
2 teaspoons ground fenugreek
2 teaspoons ground cumin
2 teaspoons turmeric powder
1 teaspoon ground cinnamon
$\frac{1}{2}$ teaspoon ground cardamom
$\frac{1}{4}$ teaspoon ground cloves
$\frac{1}{4}$ teaspoon ground nutmeg
1 teaspoon mild chilli powder
1 teaspoon freshly ground black pepper
$\frac{1}{2}$ teaspoon salt
1 small piece fresh root ginger, grated
juice of 1 lemon
2 small onions, minced
2 cloves garlic, crushed
100 g/4 oz desiccated coconut
250 ml/8 fl oz boiling water
1 (2.25-kg/5-lb) oven-ready duck

Mix all the spices and seasonings together in a mixing bowl with the ginger, lemon juice, onion and garlic. Soak the coconut in the boiling water for 5 minutes then add to the spice mixture. Stir well to make a thick paste.

Split the duck open through the breastbone and open out flat. Secure flat with skewers if necessary. Spread the paste generously over the duck and roast in a moderately hot oven (190°C, 375°F, Gas Mark 5) for $1\frac{1}{2}$ hours, or over medium coals on a barbecue for about $1\frac{1}{2}$–2 hours. Turn and baste from time to time. Serve at once with a crisp salad.

Picnic pie

PASTRY
275 g/10 oz wholemeal flour
pinch of salt
70 g/2½ oz margarine
70 g/2½ oz lard
4 tablespoons cold water
beaten egg to glaze
FILLING
2 large chicken portions
25 g/1 oz fresh white breadcrumbs
grated rind of 1 lemon
pinch of dried thyme
1 tablespoon chopped parsley
1 large onion, chopped
3 rashers lean bacon, rind removed and chopped
50 g/2 oz mushrooms, chopped
salt and freshly ground black pepper
4 tablespoons cold water

To make the pastry, place the flour in a bowl with the salt. Add the margarine and lard, cut into small pieces, and rub in with the fingertips until the mixture resembles fine breadcrumbs. Add the water and mix to a stiff dough. Divide the pastry in half and roll out one piece on a lightly floured surface large enough to line a deep 20-cm/8-inch pie plate.

To prepare the filling, remove the skin from the chicken portions, cut the chicken flesh away from the bone and divide into small pieces. Place the breadcrumbs in a bowl with the lemon rind, thyme and parsley. Add the chicken. Mix the onion, bacon and mushrooms together in another bowl.

Arrange half the onion mixture over the pastry-lined plate, season generously, cover with the chicken and breadcrumb mixture then top with the remaining onion mixture. Season again and sprinkle over the water.

Roll out the remaining pastry until large enough to cover the pie plate. Dampen the pastry rim with water and cover with the pastry lid. Trim and flute the edges. Use any pastry trimmings to make pastry leaves to decorate the pie. Make a small hole in the centre of the pie to allow any steam to escape. Glaze with the beaten egg.

Bake in a moderate oven (180°C, 350°F, Gas Mark 4) for 1½ hours or until the filling is cooked. If the pastry starts to become too brown during the cooking time, cover the top with a piece of aluminium cooking foil. Serve cold with a crisp salad.

Golden wrapped eggs

350 g/12 oz pork sausagemeat
1 teaspoon dried mixed herbs
4 hard-boiled eggs, shelled
1 (368-g/13-oz) packet frozen puff pastry, defrosted
beaten egg to glaze

Mix the sausagemeat with the herbs until well blended. Divide into four portions and shape each portion around a hard-boiled egg to cover completely.

Divide the pastry into four portions and roll each piece out, on a lightly floured surface, to a 15-cm/6-inch square. Reserve any pastry trimmings. Place an egg in the centre of each square, moisten the edges of the pastry with water and wrap the pastry around the egg to completely enclose. Place, sealed edges down, on a dampened baking tray and decorate the tops with pastry leaves made from the reserved pastry trimmings. Make a small slit in the top of each to allow any steam to escape.

Glaze each pastry-wrapped egg with beaten egg and bake in a hot oven (220°C, 425°F, Gas Mark 7) for 25–35 minutes or until golden brown. Serve cold with a mixed salad.

Variation

Golden wrapped savouries
Substitute the four hard-boiled eggs in the above recipe for 75 g/3 oz grated Cheddar cheese and 3 tablespoons brown pickle. Mix the cheese and pickle together and divide into four portions. Roll the sausagemeat in the palms of your hands and when round make a hole in the centre with a floured finger. Fill the centres with the cheese mixture using a small spoon. Mould the sausagemeat around the cheese to completely enclose. Continue to prepare and bake as above.

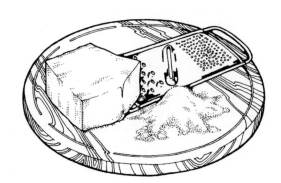

Rolled veal and ham kebabs

—— SERVES 4 ——

4 veal escalopes
4 thin slices cooked shoulder ham
1 small green pepper, deseeded
1 tablespoon French mustard
24 stuffed green olives
1 (150-g/5.3-oz) carton natural yogurt
2 tablespoons lemon juice
4 tablespoons oil
salt and freshly ground black pepper

Place the veal escalopes between two sheets of dampened greaseproof paper. Beat out until very thin. Divide each veal escalope into four pieces. Cut each slice of ham into four pieces and dice the pepper into 12 pieces.

Spread each portion of veal with the mustard, top with a slice of ham and roll up with the ham inside. Thread the veal rolls equally onto four kebab skewers, alternating with the pieces of green pepper and the olives.

Mix the yogurt, lemon juice, oil and seasoning to taste together in a small bowl. Spoon over the kebabs and allow to marinate for about 2 hours.

Cook under a moderate grill or over medium coals on a barbecue for 10–15 minutes, basting frequently with the marinade. Serve any unused marinade with the cooked kebabs.

Chicken teriyaki

—— SERVES 4 ——

4 chicken breasts
4 tablespoons dry sherry
4 teaspoons soy sauce
2 cloves garlic, crushed
2 tablespoons vegetable oil
salt and freshly ground black pepper
parsley sprigs to garnish

Remove any skin and bone from the chicken breasts and beat out until thin.

Mix the sherry, soy sauce, garlic, oil and seasoning to taste together. Spoon over the chicken and leave to marinate for about 4 hours.

Grill the chicken under a hot grill, or over hot coals on a barbecue, for 10 minutes each side, basting with the marinade from time to time.

Serve the chicken teriyaki with the remaining marinade spooned over. Garnish with parsley and accompany with new potatoes and salad ingredients.

Variations

For centuries the Japanese have cooked over charcoal. This type of cooking is called Teriyaki—teri for shiny or glazed, and yaki for grilled. Very often the food is marinated in a mixture of soy sauce, sugar, sake or sherry—so much so that it has become known as teriyaki marinade. The above marinade can also be used to cook:
Teriyaki steak: Marinate thin slices of steak then grill or barbecue for 6–10 minutes, according to taste.
Teriyaki pork: Marinate boneless pork steaks then grill or barbecue for 10–15 minutes.

Chicken in a basket

SERVES 4

4 chicken leg portions
seasoned flour to dust
1 egg, beaten
100 g/4 oz fresh white breadcrumbs
oil for deep frying
watercress sprigs to garnish

Remove the skin from the chicken portions and cut each leg in two at the joint to give eight pieces of chicken. Dust in the seasoned flour then dip lightly in the beaten egg. Roll in the breadcrumbs then chill for 1 hour to allow the coating to set.

Heat the oil to 180°C/350°F, or until a cube of day-old bread turns golden in 1 minute. Deep fry the chicken in the oil for 10–12 minutes or until cooked. Drain on absorbent kitchen paper and serve in a napkin-lined basket, garnished with sprigs of watercress.

Variation

Scampi in a basket
Just as simple to prepare and delicious to eat hot or cold is scampi in a crisp coating of breadcrumbs. Substitute the chicken portions with 450 g/1 lb large scampi. Coat in breadcrumbs and cook as above but for just 3 minutes, or until cooked through and golden.

Ranchburgers

SERVES 6

675 g/1½ lb lean minced beef
1 Spanish onion, finely chopped
1½ tablespoons Worcestershire sauce
¼ teaspoon mild curry powder
¼ teaspoon paprika pepper
salt and freshly ground black pepper
25 g/1 oz butter, softened
6 bread baps, halved and toasted

Place the beef in a bowl and mix in the onion, Worcestershire sauce, curry powder, paprika and seasoning to taste. Mix well to blend and form into six burgers. Brush with the softened butter and cook under a moderate grill or on a barbecue over medium coals for 6–8 minutes on each side.

Serve the ranchburgers between toasted bread baps. Accompany with a selection of garnishes such as spicy relishes, diced dill pickles, sliced cheese, mustard, sliced tomatoes or deep-fried onion rings.

Variations

Ranchburgers can taste doubly delicious if you top them with an additional ingredient such as:
Cheesy ranchburgers: Top the burger with a slice of quick-melting cheese.
Egg ranchburgers: Top the burger with a fried egg.
Tomato ranchburgers: Top the burger with thin slices of tomato.

Entertaining

What shall we eat today? This question generally has to be answered three hundred and sixty-five times a year by the family cook, but it seems a small problem compared with that faced by the cook who regularly entertains.

For once everything has to work extremely well and the timing must be perfect. Dishes need to be chosen with the utmost care so that they both contrast yet complement each other. When it comes to putting together the perfect menu, cooking is only half the work. The other half is the careful planning needed to achieve balance. Mix and match rich, spicy dishes with blander or subtle-tasting dishes and add accompaniments that contrast in colour, flavour and texture.

Recipes in this section include classics like *Chicken Kiev, Kidneys turbigo* and *Scallops au gratin* with the more unusual *Summertime veal escalopes, Belgian mustard beef* and *Marmalade duck.* Use these ideas with the recipes in the cook-ahead section for a never-failing repertoire of reputation-making dishes.

Filet de boeuf en croûte; Roast duckling with plum sauce (see overleaf)

Roast duckling with plum sauce

2 oven-ready ducklings, weighing about 2 kg/
4½ lb each, giblets reserved
salt and freshly ground black pepper
1 small apple, quartered
1 onion, sliced
1 lemon, sliced
1 small onion, chopped
1 carrot, chopped
1 tablespoon flour
PLUM SAUCE
1 (576-g/1 lb 4-oz) can red plums
½ bay leaf
pinch of ground nutmeg
2–3 tablespoons sugar
2 cloves
2 tablespoons vinegar

Calculate the cooking time for the ducklings, allowing 25 minutes per 450 g/1 lb. Wipe the ducklings, then sprinkle evenly with a little salt, rubbing it well into the skin. Thoroughly prick the birds all over with a fork. Mix together the apple, sliced onion and half the sliced lemon and put half into each body cavity. Place the birds, on their sides, on a grill rack in a roasting tin. Roast the ducks in a moderately hot oven (190°C, 375°F, Gas Mark 5) for 20 minutes on one side, then turn over on to the other side and roast for a further 20 minutes. After the 40 minutes, turn the birds so that they are roasting breast-side up on the rack. Reduce the oven temperature to moderate (160°C, 325°F, Gas Mark 3) and cook for the rest of the calculated cooking time.

Meanwhile, simmer the giblets with the chopped onion and carrot in about 600 ml/1 pint water and cook until the liquid has reduced to almost half. Drain and reserve the stock.

Meanwhile, prepare the plum sauce. Sieve the plums and their juice into a saucepan, add the remaining ingredients and simmer for 10 minutes.

When the ducklings are cooked remove any trussing string and place whole or carved on warmed serving plates. Tip the fat out of the roasting tin, leaving any sediment behind. Blend the flour into the sediment and cook gently until the mixture turns golden brown. Gradually add the giblet stock. Bring to the boil and season well. Keep hot to serve with the duckling. Reheat the plum sauce and strain into a serving boat. Serve the duckling topped with a little plum sauce, a few thin slices of lemon and the gravy.

Filet de boeuf en croûte

1 (900-g/2-lb) fillet of beef, about 20–23 cm/
8–9 inches long
salt and freshly ground black pepper
50 g/2 oz butter
1 tablespoon oil
225 g/8 oz pâté de foie
1 (368-g/13-oz) packet frozen puff pastry,
defrosted
beaten egg to glaze

Place the meat on a board and, using a sharp knife, trim off any excess fat. Sprinkle liberally with seasoning to taste. Tie some fine string around the meat at intervals to secure a neat shape.

Heat half the butter with the oil in a frying pan and fry the meat on all sides quickly until brown. Place in a roasting tin and dot with the remaining butter. Cook in a moderately hot oven (200°C, 400°F, Gas Mark 6) for 10 minutes. Remove, leave until cold and then remove the string.

Season the pâté to taste and beat until smooth. Using a small palette knife, spread the pâté over the top and sides of the beef.

On a lightly floured surface roll out the pastry to about 3 mm/⅛ inch thickness, into a rectangle large enough to completely enclose the meat. Place the meat, pâté side down, on the centre of the pastry. Spread the remaining pâté over the rest of the meat. Brush one long side of the pastry with beaten egg. Fold the unbrushed side over the meat, fold up the second side and press firmly together. Trim the ends of the pastry at an angle, cutting it straight off close to the meat and secure like a parcel. Reserve the trimmings for decoration. Brush the upper surfaces of the trimmed ends with beaten egg and fold diagonally across the ends like a parcel. Decorate with the pastry trimmings and glaze with the beaten egg.

Increase the oven temperature to hot (220°C, 425°F, Gas Mark 7) and bake for 40 minutes until the pastry is well risen and golden. Serve thickly sliced.

Variation

Filet de porc en croûte
A more economical dish but just as tasty! Substitute the beef fillet for three small pork fillets of the same length and tie together to form one large fillet. Prepare as above taking care to re-form the pork fillets on the pastry when the string has been removed. Bake as above for 1¼–1½ hours, covering the pastry with foil should it become too brown during cooking.

Chicken Kiev

SERVES 4

1 large clove garlic, crushed
1 tablespoon chopped parsley
100 g/4 oz butter
salt and freshly ground black pepper
4 chicken breasts, skinned and boned
1 egg, beaten
100 g/4 oz dried white breadcrumbs
oil for deep frying

Place the garlic, parsley and butter in a small bowl and mix well to blend. Season to taste. Chill in a long roll wrapped in greaseproof paper until required.

Flatten the chicken breasts between two sheets of dampened greaseproof paper until very thin. Divide the butter mixture into four portions and place in the centre of each piece of chicken. Wrap the chicken around the butter and sew up with cotton (leaving a long piece of thread so that the cotton may be retrieved after cooking).

Dip the chicken parcels in egg and then crumbs and chill to set. Heat the oil to 180°C/350°F, or until a cube of day-old bread turns golden in 1 minute. Deep fry the chicken for 5–8 minutes. Remove the cotton and serve at once with a variety of salad ingredients.

Kidneys turbigo

SERVES 4

50 g/2 oz butter or margarine
4– 6 lamb's kidneys, cored and halved
4 chipolata sausages, halved
150 ml/$\frac{1}{4}$ pint red wine
150 ml/$\frac{1}{4}$ pint stock or water
1 teaspoon tomato purée
salt and freshly ground black pepper
1 bay leaf
6–8 button onions
100 g/4 oz mushrooms, sliced
1 tablespoon flour
1 tablespoon Madeira or sherry
chopped parsley to garnish

Melt half the butter or margarine in a heavy-based frying pan and, when foaming, add the prepared kidneys and sausages. Cook until brown on all sides, remove from the pan and keep warm.

Add the wine to the pan sediment, bring to the boil and allow to reduce slightly. Stir in the stock or water, tomato purée, seasoning to taste and the bay leaf. When well mixed add the cooked kidneys and sausages, the button onions and mushrooms. Cover the pan and allow to simmer for 20 minutes.

Remove from the heat. Mix the remaining butter with the flour to make a paste. Drop into the meat stock, piece by piece, to thicken the stock. Add the Madeira or sherry. Remove the bay leaf. Garnish with chopped parsley and serve.

Southern honey-spiced ham

SERVES 8–10

1 (2.5-kg/5½-lb) middle gammon joint
2 bay leaves
1 onion, peeled and stuck with 2 cloves
1 litre/1¾ pints dry cider
3 tablespoons soft brown sugar
1 teaspoon ground cinnamon
½ teaspoon ground nutmeg
2 tablespoons clear honey
cloves (optional)

Soak the gammon joint overnight if possible, otherwise immerse in cold water in a large saucepan, bring slowly to the boil then discard the water. Drain the ham and place in a large saucepan with a close-fitting lid. Tuck the bay leaves around the ham, add the onion, cider and enough water to cover. Bring to the boil, cover then simmer very gently for 2 hours.

Lift the ham from the stock and place in a roasting tin. Mix the brown sugar with the spices and honey to form a paste. As soon as the ham is cool enough to handle, strip away the skin neatly, score the fat diagonally into a diamond pattern and rub in the honey paste. Pour the cooking stock around the ham to a depth of about 5 mm/¼ inch. Stud the ham with cloves if used. Bake in a moderately hot oven (190°C, 375°F, Gas Mark 5) for 20–30 minutes or until the coating looks crisp and golden, basting from time to time. Serve hot or cold with seasonal vegetables.

Easy beef stroganoff

SERVES 4

675 g/1½ lb rump steak
3 tablespoons seasoned flour
50 g/2 oz butter
1 onion, thinly sliced
225 g/8 oz button mushrooms, sliced
salt and freshly ground black pepper
300 ml/½ pint double cream
4 teaspoons lemon juice
GARNISH
tomato quarters
parsley sprigs

Beat the steak, trim and cut into small matchstick strips. Coat in the seasoned flour. Fry the meat in half the butter until golden brown, about 5–7 minutes. Cook the onion and mushrooms separately in the remaining butter for 3–4 minutes. Season to taste and add the cooked steak.

Mix the cream with the lemon juice and warm gently in a small saucepan. Stir the warmed cream mixture into the meat. Serve the stroganoff garnished with tomato quarters and parsley sprigs and accompany with boiled rice and a crisp green salad.

Marmalade duck

———— SERVES 4 ————

1 (2.25-kg/5-lb) duck, giblets reserved
salt and freshly ground black pepper
1 tablespoon soy sauce
2 tablespoons Seville marmalade
1 shallot, very finely chopped
2 tablespoons unsweetened orange juice
200 ml/7 fl oz stock
1 teaspoon cornflour

Prick the duck all over with a fork and place on a rack in a roasting tin. Rub with salt and roast in a hot oven (220°C, 425°F, Gas Mark 7) for 1 hour.

Pour the fat from the duck, paint the duck skin with half the soy sauce and the marmalade. Return to the oven and cook, without basting, for 15–30 minutes, or until the skin is a good brown colour.

Meanwhile, fry the shallot in a little of the duck oil, until just pale brown. Add the chopped duck liver and fry for 2 minutes. Add the orange juice, the remaining soy sauce and the stock, and bring to the boil. Stir in the cornflour mixed with a little cold water, simmer until thickened and season to taste.

Carve the duck into joints and serve with the sauce. Accompany with vegetables in season.

Veal escalopes with ginger wine

———— SERVES 4 ————

4 (75-g/3-oz) veal escalopes
seasoned flour to dust
50 g/2 oz butter
1 teaspoon oil
100 ml/4 fl oz ginger wine
2 teaspoons lemon juice
3 tablespoons double cream
salt and freshly ground black pepper
lemon slices to garnish

Dust the veal escalopes lightly with seasoned flour. Heat the butter and oil in a heavy-based pan over a moderate heat and fry the escalopes for 5–6 minutes until golden brown on both sides. Remove with a slotted spoon, place on a heated serving dish and keep warm.

Stir the ginger wine into the pan juices and bring gently to the boil. Reduce the heat and simmer slowly for 5 minutes or until the mixture becomes syrupy. Add the lemon juice and cream and simmer for 2–3 minutes, until the sauce is a pale coffee colour. Season to taste and pour over the veal escalopes. Serve garnished with lemon slices and accompany with a mixed salad.

Belgian mustard beef

SERVES 4–6

900 g/2 lb lean braising beef
1 tablespoon seasoned flour
100 g/4 oz butter
1 tablespoon oil
3 rashers bacon, rind removed and chopped
2 large onions, sliced
2 cloves garlic, crushed
300 ml/½ pint beef stock
300 ml/½ pint brown ale
2 tablespoons Meaux mustard
2 bay leaves
salt and freshly ground black pepper
6–8 slices French bread
chopped parsley to garnish

Trim the beef and cut into bite-sized cubes. Toss in the seasoned flour until evenly coated. Heat 50 g/2 oz of the butter and the oil in a pan, add the bacon and fry until crisp. Remove with a slotted spoon and place in a 1.75-litre/3-pint casserole. Add the onion to the pan and cook until soft. Remove with a slotted spoon and add to the casserole. Cook the meat in the pan until brown and seared on all sides, adding the garlic during the last few minutes of the cooking time. Remove with a slotted spoon and add to the casserole.

Stir the beef stock into the pan juices, scraping the bottom to incorporate any meat sediment. Stir in the brown ale and 1 tablespoon of the mustard and heat gently. Pour over the meat and onion mixture. Add the bay leaves and season generously. Cover the casserole with a tight-fitting lid and cook in a moderate oven (160°C, 325°F, Gas Mark 3) for 2 hours.

Meanwhile melt the remaining butter and beat in the remaining mustard. Place in a shallow flat dish and soak the bread in this mixture on one side. Place on top of the casserole, mustard side up, and bake, uncovered, for a further 30 minutes until crisp and golden. Garnish with chopped parsley before serving.

Variation

Belgian honeyed beef
Prepare the casserole as above but substitute the Meaux mustard with 2 tablespoons clear honey. To prepare the topping, melt the butter with 2 teaspoons clear honey and soak the bread in this mixture. Place on the casserole and cook as above.

Chicken Marengo

SERVES 4

4 chicken portions
seasoned flour to coat
50 g/2 oz butter or margarine
1 tablespoon oil
8 button onions
1 clove garlic, crushed (optional)
150 ml/¼ pint dry white wine
450 g/1 lb tomatoes, peeled, deseeded and
coarsely chopped
1 bay leaf
300 ml/½ pint chicken stock
1 tablespoon tomato purée
175 g/6 oz button mushrooms
6–8 black olives
chopped parsley to garnish

Coat the chicken portions in the seasoned flour. Heat the butter or margarine and oil in a large frying pan and add the chicken. Add the onions and fry gently to turn both to a golden brown, about 10 minutes. Add the garlic and cook for a further 2–3 minutes. Pour in the wine and cook quickly to reduce by about half.

Stir in the tomatoes with the bay leaf, stock and tomato purée, cover with a lid and simmer for about 20 minutes. Add the mushrooms and black olives. Continue to simmer, uncovered, for about 10 minutes, until any excess liquid has evaporated. Sprinkle with chopped parsley and serve at once.

Cook's Tip

According to culinary history Napoleon's chef was faced with the task of providing a superb meal for his general on the field of battle during the battle of Marengo at Piedmont. He had a good many luxurious ingredients but only one cooking pot so he cooked everything together and created a dish that has won universal acclaim—Chicken Marengo. If legend is correct the recipe above has all the basic ingredients but others which are claimed to have been included are:
Crayfish: Cooked or canned and placed on top of the chicken before serving.
Eggs: Deep fried in oil and served with the chicken.
Bread: Fried in butter and oil. Sit the chicken pieces on the bread croûtes to serve.

Chestnut-stuffed turkey

—————— SERVES 8 ——————

1 (4.5-kg/10-lb) turkey
SAUSAGEMEAT STUFFING
25 g/1 oz butter
100 g/4 oz stale white bread, crusts removed and
cubed
75 g/3 oz bacon rashers, rind removed, cooked
and crumbled
450 g/1 lb pork sausagemeat
1 small onion, finely chopped
2 tablespoons chopped parsley
$\frac{1}{2}$ teaspoon dried mixed herbs
4 tablespoons stock
1 egg, beaten
salt and freshly ground black pepper
CHESTNUT STUFFING
900 g/2 lb chestnuts, skinned
25 g/1 oz butter
2 tablespoons stock

Free the skin from the breast of the turkey by working
your hand down under the skin from the neck end.

Prepare the sausagemeat stuffing by melting the
butter in a saucepan. When foaming add the bread cubes
and toss until crisp. Add to the remaining ingredients,
season and mix well. Use to stuff the breast of the
turkey on both sides. Draw the skin back over the breast
of the bird and fasten in position with small skewers or
wooden cocktail sticks. Roll any excess stuffing into
balls and cook with the turkey.

Place the chestnuts in a small pan with the butter and
stock. Cook for 2 minutes then stuff loosely in the body
cavity.

Weigh the turkey with its stuffings and place in a
roasting tin. Roast in a moderate oven (180°C, 350°F,
Gas Mark 4) for 15 minutes per 450 g/1 lb and 20
minutes over, basting the bird from time to time. Serve
the turkey with a thin gravy.

Lamb steaks with rosemary

—————— SERVES 4 ——————

2 cloves garlic, crushed
4 (225-g/8-oz) lamb steaks
4 tablespoons olive oil
3 rosemary sprigs, chopped
salt and freshly ground black pepper
rosemary sprigs to garnish

Rub the garlic into the steaks and place in a shallow
ovenproof dish. Cover with the oil and leave to marinate
for at least 24 hours, covered.

Heat a grill to very hot. Sprinkle the steaks with
the rosemary and seasoning to taste. Grill quickly on
both sides for 6–8 minutes, or until the meat is brown
on the outside but barely pink inside. Serve at once
garnished with rosemary sprigs and accompany with
new potatoes and a cucumber and radish salad.

Variation

Lamb steaks with mint
Lamb is also delicious marinated in a mint mixture.
Combine 1 tablespoon white wine vinegar with 6 tablespoons natural yogurt and 4 tablespoons finely-chopped
mint. Season to taste and use to marinate the lamb
steaks. Cook as above.

Summertime
veal escalopes

—— SERVES 6 ——

6 (75-g/3-oz) veal escalopes
salt and freshly ground black pepper
25 g/1 oz butter
2 tablespoons oil
1 large onion, sliced
1 clove garlic, crushed
150 ml/$\frac{1}{4}$ pint dry white wine
$\frac{1}{2}$ cucumber, peeled, halved, deseeded and
sliced
450 g/1 lb firm tomatoes, peeled, quartered and
deseeded
1 tablespoon lemon juice

Trim the escalopes and beat out flat between two sheets of greaseproof paper. Season generously on both sides. Heat the butter and oil in a large frying pan and brown the escalopes, two at a time. Remove and keep warm.

Add the onion to the pan juices and fry until golden. Stir in the garlic, wine and seasoning to taste. Add the veal and simmer gently, uncovered, for 10 minutes. Remove the escalopes with a slotted spoon and arrange in a large warmed serving dish.

Boil the liquid in the pan until reduced to about 4 tablespoons. Add the cucumber and cook, stirring, for 5 minutes. Stir in the tomatoes and lemon juice and cook for 2 minutes. Adjust the seasoning if necessary then spoon over the escalopes. Serve with buttered pasta.

Pigeon casserole

—— SERVES 4 ——

50 g/2 oz butter
2 large pigeons, halved
1 large onion, finely chopped
100 g/4 oz streaky bacon, rind removed and diced
1 clove garlic, crushed
40 g/1$\frac{1}{2}$ oz flour
300 ml/$\frac{1}{2}$ pint stock
150 ml/$\frac{1}{4}$ pint unsweetened orange juice
1 tablespoon black treacle
1 tablespoon tomato purée
$\frac{1}{2}$ teaspoon dried thyme
100 g/4 oz mushrooms, sliced
salt and freshly ground black pepper
orange slices to garnish

Melt the butter in a flameproof casserole and brown the pigeons on all sides. Remove with a slotted spoon and set aside. Add the onion, bacon and garlic and cook for 5 minutes until lightly coloured. Shower in the flour and cook for 1 minute. Gradually stir in the stock and orange juice. Add the treacle, tomato purée, thyme, mushrooms and seasoning to taste. Mix well to blend.

Return the pigeon halves to the casserole, cover and simmer for about 1 hour or until tender. Serve garnished with quartered orange slices and accompany with rice.

Glazed salmon trout

75 g/3 oz butter
1 (2.25-kg/5-lb) salmon trout, gutted and
cleaned
2 bay leaves
600 ml/1 pint aspic jelly
a little cucumber skin, cut into matchstick
strips
a few small radishes, trimmed and thinly sliced
1 teaspoon powdered gelatine
2 tablespoons cold water
450 ml/¾ pint mayonnaise
GARNISH (optional)
watercress sprigs
cucumber slices
lemon slices

Line a large roasting tin with aluminium cooking foil. Grease the foil with 25 g/1 oz of the butter.

Wash the fish well and tuck the bay leaves inside the body cavity. Arrange the fish in the tin on its stomach (rather than laying the fish on its side) and curling from opposite corners of the tin to give a curved shape. Dot the remaining butter over the fish. Bring the edges of the foil together, without letting it touch the fish, and fold over the edges. Cook in a moderate oven (160°C, 325°F, Gas Mark 3) for 1½ hours. Baste the fish during the cooking with its own juices. Remove the fish from the oven, open out the foil and allow to cool.

When cool place the fish on a board and remove the skin, leaving the head and tail intact. Place on a serving dish and brush the fish with the liquid aspic. Arrange pieces of cucumber skin and radish slices along the side of the fish, dipping into aspic before placing on the fish. Allow to set.

Remove any aspic jelly that has collected around the base of the fish and discard. Spoon the remaining jelly over the fish and 'flood' the serving dish with a thin layer. Leave to set.

Sprinkle the gelatine on to the cold water and place over a pan of simmering water until dissolved and clear. Stir this mixture into the mayonnaise and chill for about 15 minutes until thickened.

Place the mayonnaise in a piping bag fitted with a large star-shaped nozzle and pipe a decorative design along the backbone of the fish. Garnish with watercress sprigs, cucumber and lemon slices, if liked. Serve chilled with a cucumber salad and new potatoes.

Scallops au gratin

12 scallops, cut into 2-cm/¾-inch pieces
150 ml/¼ pint dry white wine
300 ml/½ pint water
salt and freshly ground black pepper
50 g/2 oz butter
1 medium onion, finely chopped
4 tablespoons flour
4 teaspoons chopped parsley
150 ml/¼ pint single cream
675 g/1½ lb potatoes, boiled and mashed
50 g/2 oz fresh white breadcrumbs
75 g/3 oz Cheddar cheese, grated

Place the scallops in a saucepan with the wine, water and seasoning to taste. Bring to the boil then simmer for about 10 minutes or until tender. Strain and reserve 400 ml/14 fl oz of the cooking liquor.

Melt the butter in a clean saucepan. Add the onion and cook for about 5 minutes until soft. Stir in the flour and cook for 1 minute. Gradually add the reserved liquor to make a smooth sauce. Bring to the boil and simmer for 2 minutes. Add the scallops, chopped parsley and cream. Adjust the seasoning and reheat gently but do not allow to boil.

Meanwhile, pipe or spoon the potato around the edge of four flameproof dishes. Brown under the grill until golden. Spoon the scallop mixture into the centre. Mix the breadcrumbs and cheese together and sprinkle over the scallops. Lightly brown under a moderate grill and serve.

Cook's Tip

Scallops can be an expensive ingredient and are not always available fresh. Stretch half the quantity of the scallops above with 225 g/8 oz cooked, delicate white fish such as plaice, sole or flounder.

When scallops are out of season try a combination of 225 g/8 oz cooked, flaked salmon with 225 g/8 oz peeled prawns in the above sauce for a delicious alternative main dish.

Stuffed crown roast of lamb

1 (12-bone) crown roast of lamb
oil to baste
parsley sprigs to garnish
STUFFING
50 g/2 oz butter or margarine
1 medium onion, chopped
100 g/4 oz streaky bacon, rind removed and
chopped
225 g/8 oz dessert apples, peeled, cored and
finely chopped
225 g/8 oz celery, chopped
finely grated rind and juice of 1 lemon
50 g/2 oz walnuts, chopped
2 tablespoons chopped parsley
225 g/8 oz fresh white breadcrumbs
salt and freshly ground black pepper
beaten egg to bind

First prepare the stuffing. Melt the butter or margarine in a saucepan. Add the onion and bacon and cook until lightly browned. Remove from the heat and mix in the apples, celery, lemon rind and juice, walnuts, parsley, breadcrumbs and seasoning. Add sufficient beaten egg to bind the mixture.

Place the crown roast in a roasting tin and stuff the centre with the prepared mixture. (If there is too much mixture roll the excess into stuffing balls and place around the roast.) Weigh the roast and cover the bone tips with aluminium cooking foil. Roast in a moderate oven (180°C, 350°F, Gas Mark 4), allowing 30 minutes per 450 g/1 lb plus 30 minutes over. Brush from time to time with oil during cooking if the roast begins to dry.

Remove the foil tips when cooked and replace with paper cutlet frills. Garnish the roast with sprigs of parsley and serve with a gravy made from the pan juices. Accompany with redcurrant jelly and new potatoes.

Cook's Tip

If you have difficulty in obtaining a crown roast of lamb then try making your own guard of honour with the same ingredients as above. Buy a pair of six-bone racks of lamb. Using a boning knife cut away the meat and fat from the tips of the ribs. Stand the racks on end so that the ribs interlock. Pack the centre with the stuffing as above and tie string around the racks, between each rib to secure. Roast and serve as above.

Coq au vin

100 g/4 oz streaky bacon, rind removed and
chopped
40 g/1½ oz butter
12 button onions
1 (2–2.25-kg/4½–5-lb) roasting chicken, jointed
2 tablespoons brandy
450 ml/¾ pint red wine
150 ml/¼ pint chicken stock
1 bouquet garni
2 cloves garlic, finely chopped
salt and freshly ground black pepper
100 g/4 oz mushrooms
beurre manié (made from 25 g/1 oz flour mixed
with 25 g/1 oz butter)
chopped parsley to garnish

Place the bacon in a large flameproof casserole and fry, stirring constantly, until it has rendered all of its fat. Add 15 g/½ oz of the butter and fry the onions until they are golden. Transfer the onions and bacon with a slotted spoon to a plate and set aside.

Brown the chicken pieces in the pan juices on all sides until golden. Pour the brandy over and ignite. When the flames have subsided, pour in the wine and stock and add the bouquet garni, garlic and seasoning to taste. Bring to the boil, reduce the heat, cover and simmer for 1¼ hours.

Meanwhile, melt the remaining butter in a saucepan, add the mushrooms and cook gently for 2–3 minutes. Transfer to the casserole. Add the beurre manié, in small pieces, stirring constantly until the sauce has thickened. Serve at once sprinkled with chopped parsley.

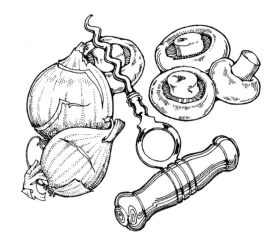

Veal à la crème flambé

SERVES 6

75 g/3 oz butter
1 (900-g/2-lb) leg of veal, boned and cut into
bite-sized pieces
1 onion
1 bouquet garni
1 clove garlic, crushed
300 ml/½ pint stock
300 ml/½ pint white wine
salt and freshly ground black pepper
225 g/8 oz button onions
1 teaspoon sugar
2 tablespoons chopped parsley
225 g/8 oz button mushrooms
beurre manié (made by mixing 40 g/1½ oz flour
with 50 g/2 oz butter)
4 tablespoons double cream
2–3 tablespoons brandy

Melt 50 g/2 oz of the butter in a flameproof casserole and cook the meat quickly to seal. Add the whole onion, bouquet garni and garlic. Pour in the stock and wine and bring to the boil. Season to taste, cover and cook in a moderate oven (160°C, 325°F, Gas Mark 3) for about 1¼ hours, until tender.

Place the button onions in a small saucepan and just cover with water. Add a pinch of salt, the sugar and remaining butter. Cook for 5 minutes, stir in the parsley and mushrooms and keep warm.

When the veal is cooked, remove and discard the onion and bouquet garni. Strain off the liquid and keep the veal warm. Reduce the liquid to 450 ml/¾ pint by rapid boiling. Stir in the beurre manié a little at a time to thicken the sauce. Add the cream. Warm the brandy and ignite. Pour over the meat. Stir the meat into the sauce. Serve the veal with the onions and mushrooms.

Chicken chasseur

SERVES 4

4 chicken portions
25 g/1 oz butter or margarine
1–2 tablespoons brandy
175 g/6 oz button mushrooms
2 teaspoons tomato purée
100 ml/4 fl oz white wine
salt and freshly ground black pepper
1 tablespoon chopped parsley to garnish
CHASSEUR SAUCE
40 g/1½ oz dripping or lard
½ small onion, finely chopped
1 small carrot, chopped
25 g/1 oz flour
450 ml/¾ pint chicken stock
1 bay leaf

Cook the chicken portions in the butter or margarine until browned on all sides. Lower the heat, cover the pan and cook for 25–30 minutes.

Meanwhile, prepare the sauce. Heat the dripping or lard in a saucepan. Add the onion and carrot and cook gently until tender and beginning to brown. Stir in the flour and cook until brown. Stir in the stock and bring to the boil. Add the bay leaf and simmer for 20 minutes.

When the chicken pieces are tender and cooked, remove the pan lid and pour over the brandy. Flame then add the mushrooms, tomato purée and white wine. Simmer for 5 minutes. Strain the chasseur sauce and pour over the chicken. Adjust the seasoning if necessary, sprinkle with parsley and serve.

Sole véronique

—————— SERVES 4 ——————

450 g/1 lb sole fillets, skinned and halved
½ teaspoon salt
½ teaspoon freshly ground white pepper
1 large onion, thinly sliced
1 bay leaf, crumbled
250 ml/8 fl oz dry white wine
3 tablespoons water
25 g/1 oz butter
25 g/1 oz flour
100 ml/4 fl oz milk
3 tablespoons double cream
225 g/8 oz green grapes, peeled, halved and
pipped

Lightly grease a large baking dish. Rub the fish fillets
with the salt and arrange on the bottom of the dish.
Sprinkle with the pepper, onion and bay leaf and pour
over the wine and water. Cover with aluminium cooking
foil and cook in a moderate oven (180°C, 350°F, Gas
Mark 4) for 15–20 minutes or until the fish flakes easily.

Remove the dish from the oven and, using a fish
slice, transfer the fish fillets to a warmed serving dish.
Strain the fish cooking liquid into a jug. Reserve
100 ml/4 fl oz of this stock.

In a small saucepan, melt the butter and stir in the
flour. Cook for 1 minute then gradually add the milk
and the reserved stock to make a sauce. Stir in the cream
and cook, stirring constantly for 2 minutes. Pour the
sauce over the fish fillets, arrange the grapes around the
dish and serve at once.

Roast goose with apple and rum stuffing

—————— SERVES 6–8 ——————

1 (4.5-kg/10-lb) goose
900 ml/1½ pints stock
100 ml/4 fl oz dark rum

STUFFING
6 large dessert apples, peeled, cored, chopped
and soaked in 4 tablespoons rum for 4 hours
¼ teaspoon dried sage
¼ teaspoon ground mace
350 g/12 oz fresh white breadcrumbs
salt and freshly ground black pepper

Place the goose on a rack in a roasting tin. Mix the
apple, sage, mace and breadcrumbs together. Season to
taste and spoon into the goose cavity. Rub salt and pepper
into the skin and then prick all over with a fork. Cover
the breast with a piece of greased aluminium cooking
foil.

Roast for 30 minutes in a moderate oven (180°C, 350°F,
Gas Mark 4). Skim off any excess fat and pour the
stock over the bird. Cook for a further 2½ hours, remove
the foil and cook for a further 1 hour so that the breast
crisps and browns.

Place the goose on a warmed serving dish. Skim away
any fat from the pan juices, reduce rapidly to make a
slightly thickened gravy.

Heat the rum in a ladle or small saucepan, pour over
the bird and flame. Serve with seasonal vegetables.

Index